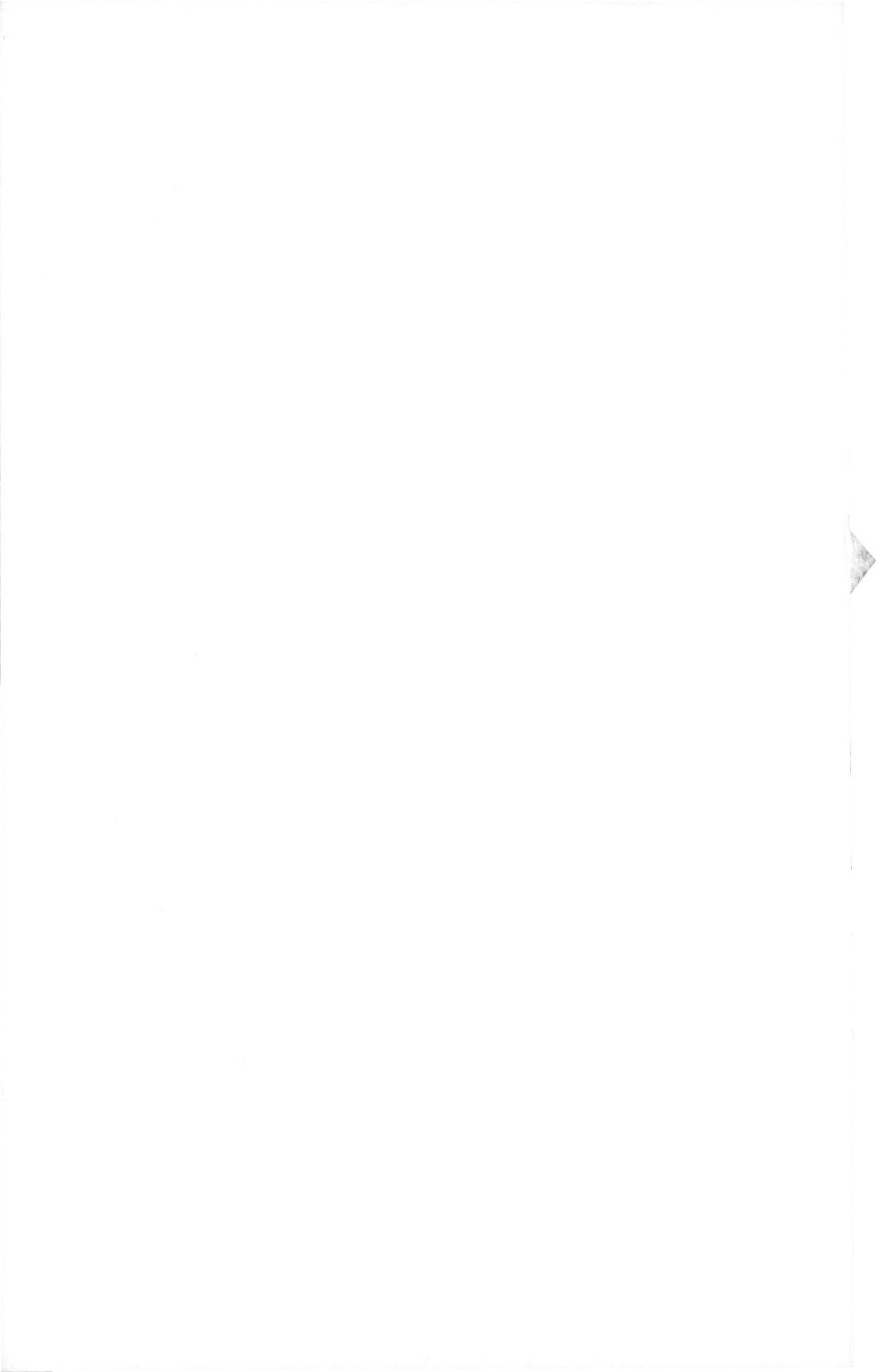

Intermediate Spanish

The Fast-Track Guide to Mastering Spanish in 30 Days

© Copyright 2022 - All rights reserved.

The content contained within this book may not be reproduced, duplicated, or transmitted without direct written permission from the author or the publisher.

Under no circumstances will any blame or legal responsibility be held against the publisher, or author, for any damages, reparation, or monetary loss due to the information contained within this book, either directly or indirectly.

Legal Notice:

This book is copyright protected. It is only for personal use. You cannot amend, distribute, sell, use, quote, or paraphrase any part, or the content within this book, without the consent of the author or publisher.

Disclaimer Notice:

Please note the information contained within this document is for educational and entertainment purposes only. All effort has been executed to present accurate, up-to-date, reliable, and complete information. No warranties of any kind are declared or implied. Readers acknowledge that the author is not engaging in the rendering of legal, financial, medical, or professional advice. The content within this book has been derived from various sources. Please consult a licensed professional before attempting any techniques outlined in this book.

By reading this document, the reader agrees that under no circumstances is the author responsible for any losses, direct or indirect, that are incurred as a result of the use of the information contained within this document, including, but not limited to, errors, omissions, or inaccuracies.

Free Bonuses from Cecilia Melero

Hi Spanish Learners!

My name is Cecilia Melero, and first off, I want to THANK YOU for reading my book.

Now you have a chance to join my exclusive Spanish language learning email list so you can get the ebooks below for free as well as the potential to get more Spanish books for free! Simply click the link below to join.

P.S. Remember that it's 100% free to join the list.

Access your free bonuses here:
https://livetolearn.lpages.co/spanish-learners/

Table of Contents:

INTRODUCTION 1
CHAPTER 1: FROM BEGINNER TO INTERMEDIATE 3
CHAPTER 2: NUMBERS, NUMBERS, NUMBERS 13
CHAPTER 3: GRAMMATICAL GENDERS 26
CHAPTER 4: FROM PERSONAL PRONOUNS TO POSSESSIVES 36
CHAPTER 5: MASTERING ADJECTIVES AND ADVERBS 52
CHAPTER 6: DEMONSTRATING HOW ARTICLES WORK 64
MID-BOOK QUIZ 73
CHAPTER 7: THE VERB I. FOCUS ON THE PRESENT 77
CHAPTER 8: THE VERB II. THINKING ABOUT THE PAST 91
CHAPTER 9: THE VERB III. TOWARDS THE FUTURE 105
CHAPTER 10: PREPOSITIONS AND CONJUNCTIONS 118
CHAPTER 11: INTERROGATIVE, AFFIRMATIVE, AND NEGATIVE SENTENCES 130
CHAPTER 12: REPORTING INFORMATION (INDIRECT SPEECH) 141
FINAL QUIZ 151
ANSWER KEY 155
HERE'S ANOTHER BOOK BY LINGO PUBLISHING THAT YOU MIGHT LIKE 173
FREE BONUSES FROM CECILIA MELERO 174

Introduction

¡Hola! ¿Cómo estás?

Are you a beginner-to-intermediate speaker of Spanish? Do you want to continue studying this fascinating language but don't have the time to take lessons? Do you get bored in a classroom? Do you think studying grammar in the abstract is hard? Do you like reading short stories? If any of this resonates with you, you've come to the right place.

Intermediate Spanish: The Fast-Track Guide to Mastering Spanish in 30 Days is a Spanish-learning book, but it's not just any book. Here, you will learn the language in a practical way thanks to our 11 Spanish short stories that will make the grammar fun and easy to understand and the exercises fun to solve.

Starting from the second one, each chapter in this book begins with a fun short story in Spanish — don't worry, we will also provide a vocabulary list for you to check the words you don't know! — that will give context to grammar topics you need to learn to advance from beginner to intermediate student. Besides, the book has plenty of quizzes and exercises for you to test how much you've learned.

To start this 30-day intermediate Spanish-learning journey, we will quickly review and quiz you on all the basic topics that you already know: the Spanish alphabet and its accents; word order in Spanish; numbers up to a hundred; the verbs *ser* and *estar*; talking about the family; regular conjugation in the present tenses;

vocabulary on food, parts of the house, and parts of the city; reading comprehension of simple texts; and writing simple descriptions.

In the second chapter, we'll study how to use numbers in Spanish in a wide range of situations, like telling the time and the date, talking about big numbers, using the cardinal and ordinal numbers, and using collective numbers.

The third chapter is dedicated to a tough topic of Spanish: gender. But don't worry; you'll learn what is the grammatical gender, the rules to determine the gender of nouns, the feminine and masculine forms of nouns and adjectives, gender agreement, and the generic masculine in Spanish. The fourth chapter is all about pronouns: personal, subject, object, demonstrative, relative, interrogative, reflexive, and possessive pronouns, among others.

We'll focus on other types of words in chapters five and six. First, we'll deepen your knowledge of adjectives and adverbs by studying adjectives used as nouns, adjectives used as adverbs, and the position of adjectives and adverbs, among other topics. Then, we'll delve into the definite and indefinite articles to tackle everything there is to know about them.

When you reach this part of the book, you'll be halfway through! So, it will be time for a Mid-Book Quiz, where you'll be tested on everything you will have learned.

Moving on, we'll have three chapters dedicated to the Spanish tenses. In chapter 7, we'll focus on the present; in chapter 8, we'll think about the past; and in chapter 9, we'll look towards the future. Chapter 10 will tackle short but important words: conjunctions and prepositions.

In chapter 11, you'll put everything learned into practice to create and organize interrogative, affirmative, and negative sentences. You'll be able to ask and answer yes/no questions, wh-questions, rhetorical questions, tag questions, polite questions, and negative statements. To finish the book, just before the final quiz, we'll talk about what other people said: we'll learn how to report information through indirect speech.

What are you waiting for? Let's embark on this 30-day journey. In this book, you'll find everything you need to continue learning Spanish and become an intermediate speaker. Let's get to it!

Chapter 1: From Beginner to Intermediate

This chapter intends to work as a bridge for you to advance from being a basic user of Spanish to an intermediate language student. With that in mind, first, we'll start with a historical and cultural overview of the Spanish language. Then, we'll move on to a basic-Spanish quiz. Afterward, we'll present a helpful tool for students of any language: the IPA chart. We'll finish off with some tips on how to best use this book.

The History of the Spanish Language

The Royal Academy of the Spanish Language tells us that the word *español* comes from the Provencal *espaignol*, which in turn comes from the Medieval Latin *hispaniolus*, meaning "of Hispania." That was the name the Romans had given to the Iberian Peninsula. This means that Spanish comes from Latin, like Portuguese, Catalan, Galician, Provencal, French, Italian, and other Romance languages. This is because most of the Iberian Peninsula was conquered by Rome and lived under its reign, like many other European territories.

In the 5th century, the fall of the Roman Empire brought a decrease in the influence of Cultured Latin among the people. Vulgar Latin was already widely spoken, a similar language but with different phonetics, syntax, and lexicon. In this context in which

Latin was losing its pure shape, the Castilian dialect was born in the Spanish region nowadays known as the Autonomous Community of Castile and León. Apart from Vulgar Latin, this first version of Spanish or Castilian had Greek, Celtic, and Germanic influences. Later, in the 7th Century, the Muslim invasion also brought its influence.

In the year 1200, under the reign of Alfonso X of Castile, the creation of a standard Spanish language based on the Castilian dialect began. The King and his court of scholars adopted the city of Toledo as the base for their activities. There, they wrote original works in Castilian, translated stories and chronicles, and scientific, legal, and literary works from other languages (mainly Latin, Greek, and Arabic). This enormous translation effort was a significant vehicle for disseminating knowledge through Ancient Western Europe. Alfonso X also adopted Castilian as the language of all administrative and official documents and decrees.

During the reign of Queen Isabella I of Castile and King Ferdinand II of Aragon, the Catholic Monarchs, the Castilian dialect was widely spread. The Monarchs completed the reconquest of Spain in 1492, after which they made Castilian the official language in their kingdom. In that same year, a very important book appeared: *Gramática de la lengua castellana* ("Grammar of the Castilian language"), by Antonio de Nebrija. It was the first treatise to study and try to define the grammar of a European language.

Just as Latin arrived in the Iberian Peninsula through conquest, the same happened with the Spanish language in the Americas. The Spanish conquerors imposed their language on the different native peoples. Through the Hispanization of the continent, Spanish was rooted as the primary language in the entire region. However, the indigenous languages greatly influenced Spanish, adding several words such as *aguacate* ("avocado"), *chocolate*, and *tiza* ("chalk") from the Aztecs; *cóndor* and *vicuña* from the Incas; and *hamaca* ("hammock") and *huracán* ("hurricane") from the Arawakan language.

All this trajectory made the resulting dialect a hybrid language that, like all languages, continues evolving, influenced by migration, mass media, science, technology, and many other factors.

Nowadays, the Spanish language is spread throughout the planet, and more than 560 million people speak it as a native, second, or foreign language. Spanish is the second language of a number of native speakers in the world, it's also second in international communications, and it's the official language of 20 countries. Being able to communicate fluently in such a universal and multicultural language is going to open lots of doors for you.

Are You an Intermediate Speaker?

This quiz is designed to test your grasp of some basic Spanish topics. Let's see how much you remember about:

- the Spanish alphabet and its accents;
- word order in Spanish;
- numbers up to a hundred;
- basic vocabulary (words for food, parts of the house, parts of the city, colors);
- talking about the family;
- the verbs *ser* and *estar*;
- common verbs conjugated in the present tenses;
- reading comprehension of a simple text;
- writing a simple description.

Are you ready? Here we go!

1. Can you write down the corresponding Spanish words for these English words? Then, spell them out loud following the example:
    a. Woman: (Mujer: eme-u-jota-e-erre)
    b. Man:
    c. Girl:
    d. Dog:
    e. House:

2. Should these words have a *tilde* (graphic accent)? Justify your answer following the example.
    a. *Cancion*: It should have a tilde in the O because it's

an *aguda* word that ends in N: *canción*.
   b. *Papel*.
   c. *Tragico*.
   d. *Esposa*.
   e. *Lapiz*.
3. What are *tildes* for?
4. What do the following words have in common? Choose the correct option: *azúcar, nunca, maleta, útil,* and *trébol*.
   a. They are all *agudas*
   b. They are all *graves*
   c. They are all *esdrújulas*
5. Is the R in *fuerza* a rolled R or soft R? What about the R in *rápido*? And the double R in *perro*?
6. Can you write down the rule for the uses of the rolled R and the soft R?
7. Choose the odd one out and justify your answer:
   a. *Agua*
   b. *Guitarra*
   c. *Merengue*
   d. *Águila*
8. All of these sentences are grammatically correct. However, there's one in each pair that is more commonly used. Can you point out which one?
   a. El libro lo escribió María.
   b. María escribió el libro.
   Los alumnos se portan mal.
   c. Se portan mal los alumnos.
   d. José preparó la cena.
   e. La cena fue preparada por José.
9. Are these sentences grammatically correct? Correct the ones that are not.
   a. Mi hermana juegan muy bien al fútbol.
   b. Tu casa nueva es muy lindo.

    c. Los niños tiene hambre.
    d. No preparé la cena.
    e. Siempre desayuno algo dulces.
    f. Mañana viene mi novia a almorzar. Le voy a cocinar pastas.
    g. Hice las compras, pero me lo olvidé en el mercado.
    h. Estoy llevando al perro al parque. Las llevo todas las mañanas.

10. True or false: In Spanish, the verb usually comes after the subject.
11. True or false: In Spanish, the subject is always explicit.
12. True or false: In Spanish, a statement's order must change to turn it into a question.
13. True or false: In Spanish, the adjectives usually go after the noun they are modifying.
14. Complete the sentence with the correct color. Remember that when colors are adjectives, they have to agree in gender and number with the noun they are modifying:
    a. El cielo es ......
    b. Las bananas son ......
    c. Las hojas de los árboles son ......
    d. La sangre es ......
    e. Las nubes son ......
    f. Si mezclas blanco y negro, obtienes ......
    g. Por fuera, el kiwi es ......
    h. Las naranjas son ......
15. Solve these calculations and write down the answers in Spanish:
    a. Dos más dos:
    b. Tres más cinco:
    c. Siete por dos:
    d. Diez más tres:
    e. Veinte menos uno:

f. Veinticinco por dos:

g. Treinta por dos:

h. Ochenta más quince:

16. Complete the sentences with the correct word for family members.
    a. El esposo de mi abuela es mi ......
    b. El hijo de mi tía es mi ......
    c. La hija de mi madre es mi ......
    d. El hermano de mi padre es mi ......
    e. Mi mamá y mi papá son mis ......
    f. La pareja de mi padre es mi ......

17. Cross the odd one out and justify your answer like in the example:
    a. *Cocina, baño, árbol, dormitorio.* Árbol, porque no es una parte de la casa.
    b. *Alfombra, sofá, cama, banana.*
    c. *Fresa, cerdo, ciruela, melón.*
    d. *Pasto, arroz, azúcar, harina.*
    e. *Sopa, habitación, cocido, pizza.*
    f. *Al horno, grillado, al vapor, blanco.*
    g. *Estrella, ayuntamiento, escuela, hospital.*
    h. *Acera, calle, semáforo, río.*
    i. *Martes, domingo, marzo, jueves.*
    j. *Viernes, octubre, abril, agosto.*

18. Match the questions on the left with what they are inquiring about on the right:

    a. ¿Cómo te llamas?   - el nombre
    b. ¿Cuántos años tienes?   - la nacionalidad/el lugar de origen
    c. ¿A qué te dedicas?
    d. ¿Tienes correo electrónico?   - la edad
    e. ¿Cuál es tu número de teléfono?   - la profesión
    - el número de teléfono
    - el correo electrónico

f. ¿Cuál es tu nombre?

g. ¿En qué trabajas?

h. ¿De dónde eres?

i. ¿Tienes móvil?

19. Complete the following card with your information:
Me llamo .... y soy (de) .... Vivo en .... Tengo .... años y soy/trabajo en .... Mi número de teléfono es .... y mi (dirección de) correo electrónico es ....

20. Complete the following sentences with *ser* or *estar*.

    a. El verbo ...... se utiliza para hablar de estados que duran mucho tiempo o son permanentes.

    b. El verbo ...... se utiliza para hablar de estados temporales.

21. Now, complete the following sentences with the present simple of *ser* or *estar*.

    a. Mi nombre ...... Alejandra.

    b. ...... de Argentina.

    c. En este momento, ... en Venezuela.

    d. Mi novia ...... de aquí.

    e. Su nombre ...... María.

    f. ...... de vacaciones juntas.

22. Complete the following chart with the conjugation of these regular verbs in the present simple:

	AMAR	**TEMER**	**PARTIR**
yo	amo	......	......
tú	......	......	partes
él / ella	......	teme	......
nosotros / nosotras	......	......	partimos

| vosotros / vosotras | amáis | ...... | ...... |
| ellos / ellas / ustedes | ...... | temen | ...... |

23. Read this short text about a Chilean-Spanish film director and answer the questions below.

    Alejandro Amenábar nace en Santiago de Chile en 1972. Al año siguiente, su familia se muda a vivir a España, a Madrid. En 1990 empieza a estudiar la carrera de Imagen y Sonido, pero no termina los estudios. En 1996 estrena su primer largometraje, Tesis.
    Poco después, llegan sus películas más famosas. Abre los ojos, *de 1997, fue un gran éxito. En 2001 se estrena* Los Otros, *una película de terror y suspenso con Nicole Kidman como protagonista.*
    En los últimos años ha filmado más películas, pero también video clips de música y series de televisión.

    a. ¿En qué año nace Alejandro Amenábar?
    b. ¿Qué edad tiene cuando sus padres se mudan a España?
    c. ¿Qué estudió en la universidad? ¿Terminó la carrera?
    d. La película que tiene como protagonista a Nicole Kidman, ¿de qué género es?
    e. ¿Qué ha hecho en los últimos años?

24. Write a short description about how you feel studying Spanish. You can use the one below as a model:
    Soy un poco tímida y me siento insegura cuando tengo que hablar en español con otras personas. En cambio, hacer los ejercicios de gramática me divierte. Soy una persona estudiosa y me gusta leer, por lo que los ejercicios de lectura y comprensión me resultan fáciles. Sin embargo, no soy buena escribiendo: todavía no aprendo las reglas de acentuación.

IPA phonemic chart

Since you already have some experience with Spanish, you probably know that Spanish pronunciation is quite different from English. However, you may also know that it's more straightforward. Once you learn how to say each letter aloud, you are pretty much set.

The IPA phonemic chart is a useful tool that can help you pronounce each letter of the Spanish alphabet. Instead of using letters, this chart uses symbols to represent the exact sound we need to make to pronounce a word. We've created one for you where you'll find the IPA symbol, then a Spanish word with that sound, and finally an English word with a similar sound. Remember that the pronunciation of the two languages is different, so the English example *is just an approximation*. When there's an X, it means there is no similar English sound.

Let's delve into this chart so that you can refer back to it in case you need help pronouncing any of this book's words.

Vocales	ä	e̞	i	o̞	u
	m*a*l	t*re*n	m*i*na	*o*ro	t*u*
	"bad"	"Ben"	"dean"	"lot"	"moon"
Consonantes	b	β	d	ð	f
	*b*ar	prue*b*a	*d*al*d*o	da*t*o	*f*uego
	"bar"	X	"dad"	"this"	"fire"
	g	j	k	l	ʎ
	*g*ato	a*y*uda*	*c*oche	*l*uz	*ll*uvia
	"game"	X	"car"	"light"	"young"
	m	n	ɲ	ŋ	p
	*m*amá	*n*ormal	*ñ*oqui	co*n*ga	*p*unto
	"mother"	"normal"	"Kanye"	"going"	"point"
	r	ɾ	s	θ	t
	*r*opa	pa*r*o	*s*ur	*z*apato*	*t*ipo
	X	"butter"**	"south"	"thought"	"type"

11

	tʃ *chocolate* "chocolate"	v *Afganistán* "vocal"	x *hoja* "hall"	ʃ *sherpa* "show"	

* This sound is not present in all Spanish dialects.
** In American pronunciation.

Hopefully, this chart will help you master Spanish pronunciation. Remember to come back to it when you have doubts about the pronunciation of any word in this book.

Tips

To finish this first chapter, we'll leave with some tips on using this book so that you can make the most of it.

As we said in the introduction, starting from chapter 2, at the beginning of each chapter, you'll find a short story. These stories are written in a level of Spanish that you'll be able to understand. However, if you have difficulty getting the gist of the text, try re-reading it a couple of times. Also, the words that can be a bit harder are **bolded** and listed below the story with their English translation. For other words you might not know, it's a good idea to try to guess their meaning from context and then check it in a dictionary. After that, we encourage you to make your own vocabulary lists or flashcards.

After each short story, there's a grammar section. There, you'll find a deep yet simple explanation for a number of topics needed to become an intermediate speaker of Spanish. We know it can be a bit overwhelming, but we've done our best to make it entertaining! So don't be afraid, and read these sections as often as you need. Sometimes, taking your own notes as you read can help the new concepts settle.

The last section in each chapter is a quiz and will cover everything in that chapter. If you don't do so well on the first attempt, we encourage you to go back to the beginning of the chapter and revise the information. Then, you can retake the quiz. Remember, practice makes perfect!

Chapter 2: Numbers, Numbers, Numbers

Short Story: Piso trece

Antes de entrar al edificio, Helena mira la **hora** en su **reloj**. Son las **nueve y veinticinco**. Llegó a su entrevista **cinco** minutos **antes**. Eso la relaja. Helena siente que esos cinco minutos le dan un **margen** de maniobra. Los necesita, porque es su primera entrevista **en mucho tiempo**. Quiere tener todo bajo control.

El lobby es un lugar elegante. El edificio es antiguo y está muy bien mantenido. Fue uno de los primeros rascacielos de la ciudad, construidos durante **la década del treinta**. Tiene **casi cien años**.

Helena se acerca al recepcionista.

—Disculpe, soy Helena Gamboa. Estoy aquí para una entrevista en el **piso trece**. Es **a las nueve y media**.

—¡Shh! —responde el recepcionista.

—¿Cómo? —pregunta Helena.

—Aquí no decimos piso tre...**Treceavo**. Es de mala suerte —aclara el recepcionista—. Pase, tome el ascensor **número dos**.

Helena decide ignorar el comentario. "Hay gente muy supersticiosa", piensa. Entonces entra en el **segundo** ascensor. Allí descubre que el edificio todavía tiene ascensorista. Es una mujer pequeña, aún más baja que Helena, con el cabello corto y blanco.

"Debe tener **por lo menos ochenta años**", piensa Helena. "Es **casi tan** vieja como el edificio". Por su expresión, la ascensorista parece estar dormida. Sin embargo, su trabajo es necesario. El ascensor no tiene botones, sino una especie de palanca ancha de bronce. No parece fácil de manipular.

—¿A qué piso? —pregunta la ascensorista.

—Al piso trece, por favor —responde Helena.

La ascensorista abre los ojos con una expresión de horror. Ya no parece estar dormida. Ahora parece aterrada.

—¡¿Qué dijo?! —pregunta la ascensorista.

—Piso trec... —responde Helena.

—Por favor, no lo repita —dice la ascensorista, mientras cubre la boca de Helena con su mano. Helena siente el olor penetrante del guante de cuero sobre su nariz—. No... Lo siento —se disculpa la ascensorista, mientras suelta a Helena—. La costumbre. Usted no sabe... Pero no tiene por qué saber. Es mejor así —se interrumpe.

Helena la mira extrañada. Sigue asustada por su reacción.

—Al **piso doce y medio**, entonces —dice la ascensorista.

Helena no responde, pero ve cómo la ascensorista maneja la palanca. En **pocos minutos** llegan a destino.

—Piso doce y medio —dice la ascensorista—. ¡Mucha suerte, señorita!

Vocabulary List

Spanish	English
la hora	time
el reloj	watch
nueve y veinticinco	twenty five past nine
cinco	five

antes	before
el margen	margin
en mucho tiempo	in a long time
la década del treinta	the 30s
casi cien años	almost a hundred years
el piso trece	thirteenth floor
a las nueve y media	at half past nine
treceavo, treceava	thirteenth
el número dos	number two
segundo, segunda	second
por lo menos	at least
ochenta años	eighty years
casi tan	almost as
el piso doce y medio	twelve and a half floor
pocos, pocas	few

Grammar Section

As we can tell from this chapter's short story, numbers are all around us! By the end of this chapter, you will be able to:

- talk about big numbers
- ask and tell the time and date
- use collective numbers
- use cardinal and ordinal numbers

Are you ready?

From cien to mil

To become an intermediate Spanish speaker, we need to be able to do more than counting to one hundred! Let's start by learning how to form big numbers. In the short story, Helena goes into a building that's almost a hundred years old (*Tiene casi cien años*). Do you know how to form numbers above *cien* ("a hundred")? For instance, "a hundred and one" is said *ciento uno*. Let's break that number down to learn how to form it. You have to add the *-to* ending after *cien*, followed by the corresponding number, in this case, *uno*.

Let's take a look at some examples:

- *Ciento tres* means "a hundred and three."
- *Ciento cinco* means "a hundred and five."
- *Ciento treinta* means "a hundred and thirty."
- *Ciento ochenta y cuatro* means "a hundred and eighty four."

After *ciento noventa y nueve* ("one hundred and ninety nine") comes *doscientos* ("two hundred"). From this number on, we add two components to the word *ciento*: a previous *dos-*, *tres-*, *cuatro-*, which indicates that we are talking about two, three, four hundred, and a final *-s* to make it plural because we are talking about more than one hundred.

Let's take a look:

- *Doscientos* means "two hundred."
- *Trescientos* means "three hundred."
- *Cuatrocientos* means "four hundred."

- *Seiscientos* means "six hundred."
- *Ochocientos* means "eight hundred."

But there are some numbers missing, right? That's because, as always, there are some exceptions.

- *Quinientos* means "five hundred."
- *Setecientos* means "six hundred."
- *Novecientos* means "nine hundred."

These last numbers don't follow the rule above, but since it's only three, I'm sure you'll remember them.

Don't forget that gender also affects numbers when we talk about hundreds. We say *cientos* when we refer to masculine things and *cientas* when we talk about feminine things. Look at the examples:

- *Helena viajó trescientos kilómetros para llegar* ("Helena traveled three hundred kilometers to get there.")
- *Había doscientas treinta y cuatro oficinas en el edificio* ("There were two hundred and thirty four offices in the building.")

Let's continue forming three-digit numbers in Spanish. After the hundred (for example, *doscientas*) comes the decimal (for example, *treinta*), followed by the word *y* plus the unit (for example, *cuatro*): *doscientas treinta y cuatro* ("two hundred and four.")

Mil and above

Do you think you can go a little further? Don't worry; the thousands and millions are quite easy in Spanish. We just need to follow the same structure as in English:

- *Tres mil* means "three thousand."
- *Cinco millones* means "five million."

And just like in English, knowing all this, you can just add as many numbers as you need. Let's see some examples:

- *Ocho mil* means "eight thousand."
- *Cuatro mil uno* means "four thousand and one."
- *Seis mil quinientos noventa y dos* means "six thousand five hundred and ninety two."
- *Cuarenta mil* means "forty thousand."

- *Ciento setenta mil* means "one hundred seventy thousand."
- *Seis millones* means "six million."
- *Once millones trescientos dos mil cuatrocientos ochenta* means "eleven million three hundred two thousand four hundred and eighty."

Let me finish the big numbers section with two differences between English and Spanish that can be quite confusing.

While English uses the comma to divide big numbers, Spanish uses a point:

- 10.900 (Spanish)
- 10,900 (English)

Knowing this, can you guess how Spanish expresses decimals? Yes, they use commas instead of points:

- 3,14 (Spanish)
- 3.14 (English)

Saying decimal numbers out loud is just like in English, but instead of saying "point", we say *coma*. So, 3,14 would be *tres coma catorce*. It can be a little confusing at first, but in the end, you just need to remember: in writing numbers, commas and points are used the other way around.

The second difference has to do with false friends, i.e., words in a language that look and sound like words in another language but that have different meanings. The Spanish *billones* does not mean the same as the English "billions". The Spanish equivalent to "billions" is *mil millones*. And *un billón* is equivalent to "trillion". So, if we wanted to talk in Spanish about the most populated country on earth, we would say:

- *China tiene **mil cuatrocientos millones** de habitantes.*

Whereas in English, we would say:

- "In China, there are **one billion four hundred million** inhabitants".

Talking about the time and the date

The most common ways to ask for the time in Spanish are the following:

- *¿Qué hora es?*, which means "What time is it?"

- *¿Tienes hora?*, which means "Do you have the time?"
- *¿Puedes decirme la hora?*, which means "Can you tell me what's the time?"

If someone asks you what's the time, or if you need to say at what time something is happening, just follow this structure:

The conjugation of the verb *ser* (*es* or *son*) + *la* or *las* + a number from 1 to 12 + *y* + the number of minutes + *de* + the part of the day

Let's see some examples:

- *Son las diez y cuarenta de la mañana* ("It's ten forty in the morning.")
- *La reunión es a la una en punto de la tarde* ("The meeting is at one o'clock in the afternoon.")

Note that for 1 a.m. and 1 p.m., we conjugate the verb *ser* in the third person singular (*es*). We do it in the plural (*son*) for all the other times of the day.

In a minute!

Just like in English, in Spanish, we divide the hours into ten-, fifteen- or twenty-minute intervals:

- *Son las doce en punto* means "It's twelve o'clock."
- *Son las tres y diez* means "It's ten past three."
- *Son las ocho y cuarto* means "It's a quarter past eight."
- *Es la una y veinte* means "It's twenty past one."
- *Son las seis y media* means "It's half past six."
- *Son las diez menos veinte* means "It's twenty to ten."
- *Son las doce menos cuarto* means "It's a quarter to twelve."
- *Son las siete menos diez* means "It's ten to seven."

What's the date?

Saying the date in Spanish is easy. Just use this structure:

Hoy es + the day of the week + the date + *de* + the month + *de* + the year

Let's see the formula applied to an example:

- *Hoy es viernes quince de julio de 2022* means "Today is Friday, July 15th, 2022."

Now, there are two differences with English worth noting. On the one hand, in English, we use ordinals, like "15th", to say the date, whereas, in Spanish, we use the cardinals, like *quince*. We only use the ordinal for *primero* ("first"). We'll talk more about cardinal and ordinal numbers in a minute. And on the other hand, as you probably already know, in Spanish, we don't use capital letters for the days of the week and the months of the year.

One or more than one?

The type of words we'll study in this section exist in English and Spanish, and "both" belong to the group! Collective numbers are used to name several persons or things as a unit, just like we did with "both" in the previous sentence. Let's see a vocabulary list with some *números colectivos*.

Spanish	English
solo	alone
el dúo, el par, la pareja	duet, pair, couple
el trío	threesome
el cuarteto	quartet
el quinteto	quintet
el sexteto	sextet
la decena	group of ten
la docena	dozen
la quincena	fortnight
la veintena	group of twenty

la cuarentena	group of forty
el centenar	hundred
el millar	thousand

The following group of collective numbers is dedicated to time periods:

Spanish	English
el trimestre	trimester
el semestre	semester
el bienio	two-year period
el trienio	triennium
el cuatrienio	four-year period
el lustro	five-year period
el sexenio	six-year period
la década	decade
el siglo	century
el milenio	millenium

Primero, el uno; segundo, el dos

We've already mentioned cardinal and ordinal numbers, and you are probably already familiar with them, even if you don't know what they are called. So, let's define them and see when we use them.

Cardinal numbers are the ones we use in counting. They indicate the number of elements in a given group. Have you guessed what we are talking about? Yes! They are just regular numbers, like *uno*, *veintidós*, and *diez*.

Ordinal numbers, as their name indicates, designate the place or order of an item in a sequence. For example, *primero*, *vigésimo segundo*, and *décimo*. Ordinals are adjectives derived from numbers, but they can sometimes work as nouns ().

The Spanish ordinals corresponding to numbers one to ten are pretty common, but Spanish speakers tend to avoid the ones above ten. For example, instead of saying *la doceava semana* ("the 12th week"), they would say *la semana doce* ("week twelve"). That's why we'll only list the most used ordinal numbers:

Spanish	English
primero, primera, primeros, primeras	first
segundo, segunda, segundos, segundas	second
tercero, tercera, terceros, terceras	third
cuarto, cuarta, cuartos, cuartas	fourth
quinto, quinta, quintos, quintas	fifth
sexto, sexta, sextos, sextas	sixth
séptimo, séptima, séptimos, séptimas	seventh
octavo, octava, octavos, octavas	eighth

noveno, novena, novenos, novenas	nineth
décimo, décima, décimos, décimas	tenth

As you can see from the table above, each Spanish ordinal has four variants. That's because ordinals are adjectives, so they vary in gender and number to match the noun they are modifying. One last thing worth noting about ordinals is that when *primero* and *tercero* are placed before a singular masculine noun, they become *primer* and *tercer*, like in the following example:

- *Mañana es mi primer día de trabajo en el nuevo puesto* ("Tomorrow is my first day of work in the new position.")

Exercises

1. Answer the following calculations by writing the numbers in Spanish - as shown in the example. These are the names of the basic operation you'll need: *más* ("plus"), *menos* ("minus"), *por* ("times"), and *dividido* ("divided").

    a. 100 + 35: *Cien más treinta y cinco es ciento treinta y cinco.*
    b. 560 - 20:
    c. 10.100 + 4.700:
    d. 225 x 6:
    e. 1.000.000 % 2,5:

2. The following chart shows the annual sales of three items in three given years. Look at it and complete the sentences, as shown in the example.

Ventas

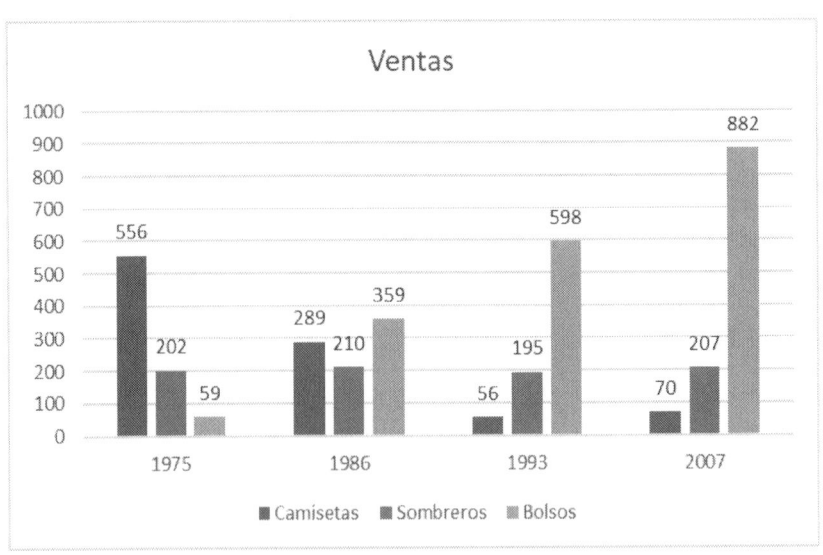

Año	Camisetas	Sombreros	Bolsos
1975	556	202	59
1986	289	210	359
1993	56	195	598
2007	70	207	882

a. *En el año mil novecientos setenta y cinco, se vendieron quinientos cincuenta y seis camisetas, doscientos dos sombreros y cincuenta y nueve bolsos.*

b. En el año .... (1986), se vendieron .... (289) camisetas, ... (210) sombreros y .... (359) bolsos.

c. En el año .... (1993), se vendieron .... (56) camisetas, ... (195) sombreros y .... (598) bolsos.

d. En el año .... (2007), se vendieron .... (70) camisetas, ... (207) sombreros y .... (882) bolsos.

3. Looking at the chart above, decide whether the following statements are true or false. Correct the false ones.

   a. En el año 1975 se vendieron más bolsos que sombreros.
   b. Se vendieron más bolsos en 2007 que en 1993.
   c. En 1986 y 2007 se vendió casi la misma cantidad de sombreros.
   d. El año en el que más bolsos se vendieron fue 1993.

4. Go back to the short story and read it again. Pay special attention to any references to time. Then, answer these questions in Spanish.
   a. What time is it when the narration starts?
   b. How early is Helena?
   c. At what time is the interview?
5. Read the following text in which someone is talking about their routine:
   a. *De lunes a viernes, me levanto a las siete y media de la mañana. Comienzo a trabajar a las nueve. Entre las doce y cuarto y la una del mediodía, me tomo un descanso para almorzar. Termino de trabajar a las cinco de la tarde. A las ocho y media, ceno. Me acuesta sobre las diez y media u once de la noche.*
   b. Now, write a similar text describing your routine. Make sure you include when you wake up, start work, have lunch, finish work, have dinner, and go to bed.

Congratulations on the good work! Now that you've finished the chapter, you can go back to the beginning of the grammar section and tick the topics you think you've learned.

Chapter 3: Grammatical Genders

Short Story: Alicia y la coneja

De pronto, Alberto deja de caminar. Silvia **avanza** un paso más, hasta que él le hace un gesto con la mano. Entonces ella también **se detiene**.

—Mira —dice Alberto **en voz baja**. **Señala** hacia adelante.

Silvia sigue la indicación de Alberto. Es de noche, y no hay nadie más en esa zona de la ciudad. Es un barrio comercial. De noche, las tiendas cierran y casi no hay tránsito.

—¿Qué pasa? —pregunta Silvia, intrigada.

—Un conejo —responde Alberto.

Entonces Silvia lo ve. Delante de un **cubo de basura, en plena calle**, hay un conejo blanco. Es grande. Parece suave y muy limpio.

—No lo puedo creer —dice Silvia.

—¿Un **conejo**, en la ciudad? —contesta Alberto.

—Bueno, quizás es una **coneja** —dice Silvia.

—No sé si eso es lo realmente importante —responde Alberto. Está sorprendido por la situación.

—Es muy grande —continúa Silvia—. Tiene el tamaño de un perro. ¿Los conejos son **más grandes** que las conejas? ¿O es **al** revés?

—No tengo ni idea —dice Alberto.

—¿Qué hace aquí? —pregunta Silvia—. En este barrio, esperaba ver palomas. Esas **palomas** feas que andan por la ciudad. O **ratas**.

—¿Cómo sabes que no son **palomos**? —contesta Alberto, **juguetón**—. O **ratones**.

—Creo que las ratas y los ratones son animales distintos —dice Silvia.

—Mira, se mueve —contesta Alberto.

El conejo (o la coneja) da unos saltos hacia el frente. Es bastante rápido (o rápida).

—¡Sigámosla! —dice Silvia.

Ambos avanzan detrás del conejo (o la coneja). Mantienen una **distancia segura** para no asustarlo (o asustarla). Sin embargo, la aventura no dura mucho tiempo. A los pocos metros, una niña **recoge** al animal. Ella está delante de la puerta de una casa vieja. Detrás, la espera su madre.

—¡Terminó el paseo! —dice la niña cuando recoge a su **mascota**.

—¿El conejo es tuyo? —pregunta Alberto.

—Es una coneja —responde la niña.

—¡Te lo dije! —dice Silvia.

—¿Cómo se llama? —pregunta Alberto, sin darle importancia a lo que dice su amiga.

—Blanquita —dice la niña.

—Es un nombre muy apropiado —responde Alberto—. Ella es en verdad muy blanca.

—¡Alicia, entra ya! —grita la madre, desde el interior de la casa—. ¿Qué te dije de hablar con **desconocidos**?

Vocabulary List

Spanish	English
de pronto	suddenly
avanzar	move forward
detenerse	stop
en voz baja	in a low voice, whispering
señalar	point at
el cubo de basura	trash can
en plena calle	in the middle of the street
el conejo	rabbit
la coneja	doe
más grande	bigger
al revés	the other way around
la paloma	pigeon
la rata	rat
el palomo	cock pigeon
juguetón, juguetona	playful

el ratón	mouse
distancia segura	safe distance
recoger	pick up
la mascota	pet
el desconocido, la desconocida	stranger

Grammar Section

By now, you probably know that Spanish is a gendered language. While English only shows gender in personal pronouns, in Spanish, everything has gender. Even animals, as we can tell from the story above! But, what *is* gender? Well, in this chapter, we'll tackle that question, together with the following subjects:

- what is the grammatical gender
- the rules for determining the gender of words
- the feminine and masculine forms of nouns and adjectives
- gender agreement
- referring collectively to masculine and feminine nouns

Are you ready? Let's get to it!

Grammatical gender

Grammatical gender is a property of languages. It's used to divide nouns, pronouns, and adjectives (i.e., nominal elements) into classes. In Spanish, there are two grammatical genders: masculine and feminine. Some languages have more, like German, which has three (masculine, feminine, and neuter), and other languages don't have this distinction. In English, for example, there's no gender agreement between nominal elements, and gender is only reflected in pronouns referring to people.

So, Spanish is a gendered language. But, what does it mean? It means that all nouns have gender and that the pronouns, articles, and adjectives around nouns have to reflect that gender. This is what we call agreement or concord: the need to change a word to make it match a grammatical feature of another word to which it's syntactically connected.

It sounds confusing, doesn't it? But let's take an example of agreement from English so that you can get the gist of it. In English, there is agreement between demonstratives and nouns: the number of a noun determines which demonstrative we are going to use. So, with a singular noun such as "car," we need a singular demonstrative. We say "this car" or "that car." If we take that same noun in its plural form, we must use a plural demonstrative. We say "these cars" or "those cars." See? It wasn't so hard.

Now that we understand the concept of agreement, we need to take it to Spanish, where every word related to a noun has to agree in gender and number with that noun, and where all nouns have gender. Even though it might sound weird to you, *mesa* ("table") is feminine, and *coche* ("car") is masculine. Furthermore, if we used those nouns with an article, we would say *la mesa* ("the table") and *el coche* ("the car"). So, *la* is the definite article (equivalent to English "the") that comes before feminine nouns, and *el* is the one for masculine ones. This is important to remember. Throughout this book, we always put an article together with a noun in the vocabulary lists so that you can know the gender of the word if it's not that clear.

Now let's talk about why some nouns are feminine and others masculine. It has to do with the word's etymology, the language's evolution, and other more complicated causes. However, in order to be fluent in Spanish, you don't need to go back in history. All you need to know is whether the noun is masculine or feminine; we'll help you with that in the next section.

Feminine or masculine?

Establishing the gender of a noun is not easy, but some concepts will help you. The first rule is that nouns referring to women tend to be feminine, and nouns referring to men tend to be masculine. Let's see some examples:

- *La mujer* is "the woman."
- *La niña* is "the girl."
- *La hija* is "the daughter."

- *La hermana* is "the sister."
- *La prima* is "the female cousin."
- *La tía* is "the aunt."
- *El hombre* is "the man."
- *El niño* is "the boy."
- *El hijo* is "the son."
- *El hermano* is "the brother."
- *El primo* is "the male cousin."
- *El tío* is "the uncle."

You can probably infer the second rule from going back to the examples above and paying attention to the last letter of all the words. Can you draw any conclusions?

In the nouns we listed, all the feminine ones end in -A, and almost all the masculine ones end in- O. Although the sample is not representative of the language, we can say that most nouns ending in -A are feminine and that most nouns ending in -O are masculine. However, as with any rule, there are many exceptions. For example, *la foto* ("the photo") is feminine, and *el programa* ("the program") is masculine. Besides, there're plenty of nouns that end in other letters, like *el hombre*, above.

Other typically masculine endings are -MA, like in *el pijama* ("the pajama"), and -OR, like in *el olor* ("the smell"). On the other hand, there are some other feminine endings besides -A. Nouns ending in -SIÓN, -CIÓN, -DAD, -TAD, -TUD, or -UMBRE are always feminine. Some examples are *la confusión* ("the confusion"), *la acción* ("the action"), *la soledad* ("the loneliness"), *la libertad* ("the freedom"), *la juventud* ("the youth"), and *la costumbre* ("the habit").

As you can see, there are some rules, but there are also many exceptions. Our recommendation: try to learn each new noun together with its article so that you can be sure of its gender.

How to form feminine and masculine words

It's time to talk about morphemes! Morphemes are the minimum unit carrying meaning within a word. To form words, we take the root (for example *herman-*) and add morphemes: -O and -

A to indicate gender, and -S to indicate number.

So, to indicate gender, we follow this process:

- herman + o = hermano ("brother").
- herman + a = hermana ("sister").

And, to indicate number:

- *herman + o + s = hermanos* ("brothers" or "siblings," because of the generic masculine, a concept we will see in a following section).
- *herman + a + s = hermanas* ("sisters").

These changes, called nominal flexions, apply to nouns and also adjectives. Let's see what happens with *lindo/linda* ("cute"):

- *lind + o: lindo* ("cute" used to describe masculine nouns).
- *lind + a: linda* ("cute" used to describe feminine nouns).

And let's see gender combined with number:

- *lindo + s: lindos* ("cute" used to describe plural, masculine nouns).
- *linda + s: lindas* ("cute" used to describe plural, feminine nouns).

Let's see some examples:

- *Mi hermano es lindo* ("My brother is cute.")
- *Mis hermanas son lindas* ("My sisters are cute.")

Gender agreement: How does it work?

We have explained how gender works at the lexical level, that is, what happens with words. Now it's time to talk about what happens with gender throughout the sentence: we need to talk about agreement. We'll use some examples to show you how concord works:

- *La casa amarilla estaba alta* ("The yellow house was high.")
- *El barco amarillo estaba hundido* ("The yellow boat was sunk.")

As we already established, in Spanish, everything regarding gender is determined by nouns. In the examples above, all the bolded words express gender in agreement with the nouns, which are underlined.

When we talk about *casa*, a feminine noun, the article (*la*) and the adjectives that modify it (*amarilla* and *alta*) must also be feminine. The same would happen if we used a pronoun to replace the feminine noun *casa*, like in the following examples:

- ***La** casa **amarilla** estaba **alta**. Nos costó llegar a **ella*** ("The yellow house was high. It was hard to get to it.")

The same applies when we talk about *barco*, a masculine noun. We can see how the article (*el*), and the adjectives (*amarillo* and *hundido*) are also in the masculine. And what would happen if we used a pronoun to replace de masculine noun *barco*? Let's see:

- ***El** barco **amarillo** estaba **hundido**. Debieron descender mucho para dar con **él*** ("The yellow boat was sunk. They had to descend a lot to reach it.")

The examples above show us graphically how gender is spread throughout the sentence, affecting all the articles, adjectives, and pronouns connected to a noun. It may look a little overwhelming, but don't worry! You'll get the hang of it in no time.

Generic masculine

As we said, Spanish has two genders that determine much of what happens in speech. On the one hand, masculine nouns take masculine articles and adjectives and are replaced by masculine pronouns. On the other hand, feminine nouns take feminine articles and adjectives and are replaced by feminine pronouns. But, what happens when we have a group that includes masculine and feminine nouns? We'll talk about that in this section.

- *Juan tiene tres hijas: Sofía, Clara y María* ("Juan has three daughters: Sofía, Clara and María.")

- *Carlos tiene dos hijos: Manuel y Pedro* ("Carlos has two sons: Manuel and Pedro.")

- *Mario tiene dos hijos: Joaquín y Mónica* ("Mario has two children: Joaquín and Mónica.")

Let's take a closer look at these examples. In the first case, Sofía, Clara, and María are three girls; that's why we say that Juan has three *hijas* ("daughters"). In the second case, Manuel and Pedro are two boys, so it makes sense to say that Carlos has two *hijos* ("sons").

But what happens in the last case? Joaquín is a boy's name, and Mónica is a girl's name, so we can assume that Mario has a son and a daughter. However, we say he has two *hijos*, in the masculine.

What we've just described is called *masculino genérico* ("generic masculine"). This means that whenever we refer to mixed groups of people, animals, or things (i.e., groups that include feminine and masculine nouns), we use the masculine as generic. This is true both for the nouns and the adjectives. Let's check out some examples:

- *Mi madre tiene cuatro nietos: un niño y tres niñas* ("My mother has four grandchildren: one boy and three girls.")

We can see how *nietos* includes both the three granddaughters and the grandson.

- *Las casas y los edificios de esta ciudad son muy bellos* ("The houses and the buildings in this city are very beautiful.")

Here, *bellos* (masculine) is describing both *las casas* (feminine) and *los edificios* (masculine).

With that, we've covered everything you need to know about gender to be an intermediate student. Now, let's put it into practice through some exercises!

Exercises

1. Go back to the short story at the beginning of the chapter and answer the following questions in Spanish.
    c. ¿Por dónde están caminando Silvia y Alberto?
    d. ¿En qué momento del día transcurre la historia?
    e. ¿Qué animales se mencionan en la historia?
    f. ¿Por qué la aventura de seguir a la coneja no dura mucho?
2. Decide whether the following statements are true or false. Correct the false ones.
    a. Grammatical gender has to do with the gender of people.

b. There are languages that have no grammatical gender.

c. In Spanish, there are no grammatical genders.

d. Agreement is the need to change a word to make it match a grammatical feature of another word.

3. Complete the sentences with these endings: -TUD; -OR; -SIÓN; -A; -MA; -O. Provide an example of each.

   a. Most nouns ending in ... are feminine, for example ......

   b. Most nouns ending in ... are masculine, for example ......

   c. Other typically feminine endings are ... (for example: ......), and ... (for example: ......)

   d. Other typically masculine endings are ... (for example: ......), and ... (for example: ......)

4. Choose the correct article, adjective, or pronoun to match the gender of the main noun: *Mi nombre es Soledad. Mi lugar ...... (favorito/a) de ...... (el/la) casa es mi habitación. Allí paso ...... (el/la) tiempo libre. Me gusta escuchar música, leer ...... (muchos/as) libros y dibujar. Me siento muy ...... (cómodo/cómoda) en mi habitación. Al entrar por ...... (el/la) puerta se ve al fondo ...... (el/la) ventana, que deja entrar ...... (un/una) luz ...... (claro/clara). Las paredes están ...... (pintados/pintadas) en un tono ...... (oscuro/oscura). La cama es muy ...... (cómodo/cómoda). Encima de ...... (él/ella), hay un poster de mi banda ...... (preferido/preferida). Al lado de ...... (el/la) cama hay ...... (un/una) armario. En ...... (él/ella), guardo mi ropa bien ...... (doblado/doblada).*

5. Write a short description of your favorite room following the model above (around 100 words).

Chapter 4: From Personal Pronouns to Possessives

Short Story: Una familia tradicional

Casandra **estaciona** el coche y apaga el motor. Desde su asiento, mira primero a la casa de sus padres, y después a Guadalupe. Ella sonríe desde el **asiento del acompañante**.

—Mira, Lupe —dice Casandra, **titubeando**—. Mi familia es... ¿cómo decirlo? Especial.

—Todas las familias son especiales —contesta Guadalupe con una sonrisa.

—Sí, eso es cierto, pero... —dice Casandra—. Tú solo tienes que **seguirles la corriente**, ¿sabes? Yo los quiero, pero son... difíciles.

—No creo que haya problema —responde Guadalupe.

—¿Recuerdas quiénes estarán en el almuerzo de hoy? —pregunta Casandra.

—Creo que sí —dice Guadalupe—. Tus padres, por supuesto. Tu hermano, Héctor. Tus tíos, Aquiles y Alejandro. Y tu abuela... ¿Cómo se llamaba?

—Mi abuela se llama Circe —dice Casandra.

—¡Eso, Circe! —contesta Guadalupe—. Es un nombre extraño. Por eso no lo recordaba.

—Ya sabes, es nuestra tradición —dice Casandra—. Todos tenemos nombres salidos de la *Ilíada* y la *Odisea*. Mi **bisabuelo** era griego, y estaba muy orgulloso de serlo.

—¿Ese es el que hizo un viaje de doscientos kilómetros **a pie**? —pregunta Guadalupe.

—No, esos fueron mis padres —responde Casandra—. Fue su **luna de miel**. Mi bisabuelo es el que hablaba **en verso**.

—¿En verso? —pregunta Guadalupe.

—**Rimando** —responde Casandra, **encogiéndose de hombros**—. Ya te dije, son todos muy originales.

—Me parece que exageras —dice Guadalupe.

Casandra **suspira**, gira sobre su asiento y mira a Guadalupe a los ojos.

—¿Qué hace tu familia en Navidad? —pregunta Casandra.

—**Pues**... Nos juntamos en casa de mi abuela —responde Guadalupe—. Cocinamos, comemos. Nos peleamos, por supuesto. Esta última vez, el primo de mi madre, Sebastián, hizo unos comentarios horrorosos sobre la **herencia** de su tía Gladys.

—Me contaste, lo recuerdo —dice Casandra—. Estuvo **fuera de lugar**. Pero suena bastante normal. Nosotros, en cambio, hacemos un torneo de **tiro con arco**.

—¿Sabes tirar con arco y flecha? —pregunta Guadalupe, entusiasmada.

Casandra mira a Guadalupe y ve la emoción en sus ojos. Cualquiera diría que está lista para empezar sus lecciones de tiro. Eso le **arranca una sonrisa**. Entonces mira su reloj y ve que ya es hora de entrar.

—Sí, y de hecho soy la campeona **vigente** —contesta Casandra—. Cuando quieras, te enseño.

—Encantada —dice Guadalupe.

—¿Estás lista, entonces? —pregunta Casandra.

—Por supuesto —responde Guadalupe.

—Vamos —dice Casandra, y abre la puerta del coche.

Vocabulary List

Spanish	English
estacionar	park
el asiento del acompañante	passenger seat
titubear	hesitate
seguir la corriente	go along with
el bisabuelo	great-grandfather
a pie	on foot
la luna de miel	honeymoon
en verso	in verse
rimar	rhyme
encogerse de hombros	shrug one's shoulders
suspirar	sigh
pues	well
la herencia	inheritance
fuera de lugar	inappropriate
el tiro con arco	archery

arrancar una sonrisa	make somebody smile
vigente	current

Grammar Section

As a basic student of Spanish on your way to becoming an intermediate user of the language, you have undoubtedly encountered pronouns before, so these words are probably not new to you. However, in this chapter, we'll review the basic types of pronouns and add some more complex ones. So, by the end, you'll master:

- personal pronouns;
- subject and object pronouns;
- pronouns used with prepositions;
- reflexive pronouns and reciprocal;
- demonstrative pronouns;
- numeral pronouns;
- quantitative pronouns;
- indefinite pronouns;
- interrogative and exclamatory pronouns; and
- relative pronouns.

The list of Spanish pronouns is long, so let's get to it!

Pronouns: What are they?

The word "pronoun" comes from the Latin word *pronōmen*, meaning "instead of the name." Pronouns are the words we use to replace names or nouns in a sentence. Their function is to stand for any grammatical person mentioned—including people, animals, or things. Also, they reflect the gender (feminine, masculine or neutral) and number (singular or plural) of such person. Let's see how they work with a few examples:

- *Sara está enojada. Habla con **ella*** ("Sara is mad. Talk to her.")

In the example, the pronoun *ella* ("her") is replacing the name, Sara. As you can see, it reflects the third person singular feminine.

Pronouns also serve to refer to elements that function as antecedents of a topic. For example:

- *María es muy amable con todo el mundo. **Eso** hace que todos la quieran* ("María is very nice to everybody. That makes everyone love her.")

In this case, *eso* ("that") is standing for the whole previous sentence.

Personal pronouns

Personal pronouns designate the participants of speech. The first person refers to the speaker, the second person refers to the listener, and the third person refers to someone outside the conversation. Spanish personal pronouns have different functions in the sentence, showing the relationship that participants have between them, i.e., who is the doer of the action, who is the receiver, etc. And depending on their function, they take different forms, as you can see in the table below.

		Subject	Direct Object	Indirect Object	Prepositional
Singular	1ra persona	yo	me		mí
	2da persona	tú, vos	te		ti
	2da persona	usted	la, lo	le, se	usted
	3ra persona	ella, él			ella, él

Plural	1ra persona	nosotras, nosotros	nos		nosotras, nosotros
	2da persona	vosotras, vosotros	os		vosotras, vosotros
	2da persona	ustedes	las, los	les, se	ustedes
	3ra persona	ellas, ellos			ellas, ellos

Have you noticed the *tilde* on *tú* ("you"), *él* ("he"), and *mí* ("me")? That's a diacritical accent so that they don't get mixed up with *tu* ("your"), *el* ("the"), and *mi* ("my").

Another thing worth mentioning when talking about personal pronouns is the difference between *tú*, *vos*, and *usted* ("you"), which you probably already know: *usted* is used to express respect when speaking to someone older or in a higher position. *Tú* and *vos* are both informal: the first one is used in almost every Spanish-speaking country, and *vos* is used in some Latin American countries, such as Argentina, Uruguay, Paraguay, and in regions of Chile, Bolivia, Venezuela, Costa Rica, etc.

Let's see the different forms of personal pronouns in more detail.

Subject pronouns

Personal pronouns often have the function of the subject of a sentence, that is, the author of the action of the verb. Subject personal pronouns always match the person and number of the verb. This concord between the subject and the verb is what makes possible the tacit subject in Spanish since we can infer the doer of the action from the inflection of the verb. Let's see some examples:

- *Yo tengo novia* ("I have a girlfriend." *Tengo novia* is also possible.)
- *Ella se llama Lucrecia* ("She's called Lucrecia." *Se llama Lucrecia* is also possible.)

Direct object pronouns

The direct object completes the meaning of transitive verbs; it refers to a thing or person, and a direct object pronoun can replace it.

- *Estoy comiendo una manzana* → *La estoy comiendo* ("I'm eating an apple → I'm eating it.")
- *Estoy esperando a mis padres* → *Los estoy esperando* ("I'm waiting for my parents → I'm waiting for them.")

Indirect object pronouns

The indirect object designates the recipient of the action described by the verb, which is always an animated being. Like the direct object, it can be replaced by a pronoun. When a sentence has both a direct object pronoun (*lo, la, los, las*) and an indirect object pronoun (*le, les*), the latter is replaced by *se* to avoid the cacophony.

- *María compró un regalo **a sus padres*** → *María **les** compró un regalo* → *María **se** los compró* ("María bought a present **for her parents** → María bought **them** a present → María bought it **for them**.")

Placement of direct and indirect object pronouns

Regardless of the tense, direct and indirect object pronouns go before the verb:

- *Susana **la** conoce desde hace años* ("Susana has known her for years.")
- ***Me** encanta cantar canciones* ("I love singing songs.")

If a sentence has both pronouns, the indirect object always precedes the direct object:

- *-¿Dónde compraste esa silla? -**Me la** regaló mi mamá* ("-Where did you get that chair? -My mom gave it to me.")

In sentences containing a gerund or an infinitive, the pronoun may precede or follow the entire verbal group:

- *Quiero tocar otra canción* → ***La** quiero tocar/Quiero tocar**la*** ("I want to play another song → I want to play it.")

In affirmative imperative sentences, the personal pronoun goes after the verb. In negative imperative sentences, it goes before the verb.

- *¡Lava los platos!* → *¡Lávalos!* ("Wash the dishes! → Wash them!")

- *¡No hagas eso!* → *¡No lo hagas!* ("Don't do that! → Don't do it!")

Prepositional pronouns

Prepositional personal pronouns go after prepositions (*a, con, hacia, para, por, sobre, sin,* etc.)

- *Escribo canciones para **ella*** ("I write songs for her.")

The singular first and second person pronouns *mí* and *tú* have incorporated the proposition *con*: *conmigo* ("with me") and *contigo* ("with you").

- *Me encanta escuchar música **contigo*** ("I love listening to music with you.")

Reflexive pronouns

We use reflexive personal pronouns to indicate that the action falls on the subject.

		Subject Pronoun	Reflexive Pronoun
Singular	1ra persona	yo	me
	2da persona	tú, vos	te
	2da persona	usted	se
	3ra persona	ella, él	se
Plural	1ra persona	nosotras, nosotros	nos
	2da	vosotras, vosotros	os

	persona		
	2da persona	ustedes	se
	3ra persona	ellas, ellos	se

For example:

- *Cuando Marta sale, **se** pone su mejor vestido* ("When Marta goes out, she wears her nicest dress.")
- *José **se** baña por las mañana* ("José takes a shower in the mornings.")

Reciprocal pronouns

Reciprocal pronouns (*os, nos, se*) show the reciprocity of actions between two or more subjects, that is, that the action concerns several individuals. One way of testing if a pronoun is reciprocal is adding the adverb *mutuamente* ("mutually"). For example:

- *Ramón y yo **nos** juramos lealtad eterna (mutuamente)* ("Ramón and I swore eternal loyalty to each other.")
- *Mis primos **se** llevan muy mal (mutuamente)* ("My cousins don't get along with each other.")

Possessive pronouns

They are used to express the possession of a thing by a noun. They have gender, number and person inflection (inflection is the change of form in words to mark grammatical cases). Unlike the ones in English, in Spanish, they agree with the thing that's possessed, not with the person who owns it. Let's check them out:

	Feminine		Masculine	
Owner	Singular	Plural	Singular	Plural
yo	mía	mías	mío	míos
tú, vos	tuya	tuyas	tuyo	tuyos
usted	suya	suyas	suyo	suyos
ella, él	suya	suyas	suyo	suyos
nosotras, nosotros	nuestra	nuestras	nuestro	nuestros
vosotras, vosotros	vuestra	vuestras	vuestro	vuestros
ustedes	suya	suyas	suyo	suyos
ellas, ellos	suya	suyas	suyo	suyos

If we take the first row, we can say that *mía* is the pronoun the speaker uses to talk about something that belongs to them that is feminine and singular. *Mío* is used when the thing possessed is masculine and singular; *mías*, when it's feminine and plural; and lastly, *míos*, when it's masculine and plural.

For example:
- *Estas camisetas son **tuyas** y este pantalón también es **tuyo*** ("These t-shirts are yours, and these trousers are also yours." The owner is the same person, and regardless of their gender, we use first *tuyas*, because *camisetas* is a feminine plural noun; and then *tuyo*, because *pantalón* is a masculine singular noun.

- *La decisión es **nuestra*** ("The decision is ours.")

If we want to emphasize that the possessors are different, we use the definite article.

- *Estas medias son **tuyas**. **Las mías** ya las guardé* ("These socks are yours, I've already put away mine.")

Demonstrative pronouns

Demonstrative pronouns indicate a relationship of proximity between the designated person and the other participants of the conversation.

Distance	Femenine		Masculine		Neuter
	Singular	Plural	Singular	Plural	Singular
Cerca del hablante	esta	estas	esto	estos	esto
Cerca del destinatario	esa	esas	ese	esos	eso
Lejos de ambos	aquella	aquellas	aquel	aquellos	aquello

For example:

- *¿Cuál es el precio de **aquel**?* ("What's the price of that one?")
- ***Eso** no estuvo bien* ("That was not okay.")
- *¿Encontraste tu taza? **Esta** es la mía* ("Have you found your glass? This one's mine")

Numeral pronouns

We've already talked about numbers in chapter 2. Now, we'll see how they can also function as pronouns to indicate the number of objects represented in a sentence.

Cardinals	Ordinals	Fractions	Multiples
uno, dos, tres, etc.	primero, segundo, tercero, etc.	tercio, mitad, cuarto, etc.	doble, triple, cuádruple

For example:

- *Me gustan estas rosas. Deme **doce**, por favor.* ("I like these roses. Give me twelve, please.")
- *Que pase el **primero**.* ("The first one can come in.")
- *Iba a comprar un kilo de harina, pero solo había **medio**.* ("I wanted to buy one kilo of flour, but there was only half.")
- *Hoy hicimos 500 kilómetros. Mañana deberíamos hacer el **doble**.* ("Today we did 500 kilometers. Tomorrow we should do twice as many.")

Quantitative pronouns

They represent indeterminate quantities of elements. They all vary in number, and most also vary in gender, with a couple of exceptions. Let's take a look at them:

	Singular	**Plural**
Neuter	bastante, suficiente	bastantes, suficientes
Femenine	poca, mucha, toda	pocas, muchas, todas
Masculine	poco, mucho, todo	pocos, muchos, todos

For example:

- *No te olvides de comprar agua. No tenemos **suficiente*** ("Don't forget to buy water. We don't have enough.")
- *A Victoria la agarró la lluvia en la calle. Está **toda** mojada* ("Victoria was caught in the rain in the street. She's all wet.")

- *Hace tiempo que espero, pero ya falta **poco*** ("I've been waiting for a long time, but I won't have to wait much longer.")

Indefinite pronouns

They point to an imprecise or unknown person.

	Singular	**Plural**
Neuter	cualquiera, quienquiera	cualesquiera, quienesquiera
Femenine	alguna, ninguna, otra, una	algunas, ningunas, otras, unas
Masculine	alguno, ninguno, otro, uno	algunos, ningunos, otros, unos

For example:

- *No puedes confiar en **cualquiera*** ("You can't trust anyone.")
- *Siempre usas el mismo sombrero. ¿No tienes **otro**?* ("You always wear the same hat. Don't you have another one?")
- *Les avisé a mis amigas del cambio de horario, pero **algunas** no leyeron el mensaje y llegaron tarde* ("I told my friends about the change in the schedule, but some didn't read the message and arrived late.")

Interrogative and exclamatory pronouns

They are the same words with different functions. Interrogative pronouns are used to ask questions related to identity or quantity. Exclamatory pronouns are used to emphasize the expressiveness of the statement. They are all written with a *tilde*.

	Singular	Plural
Neuter	qué, quién, cuál	quiénes, cuáles
Femenine	cuánta	cuántas
Masculine	cuánto	cuántos

For example:

- *¿**Quién** era la persona que te saludó?* ("Who was the person who said hi?")
- *¿**Cuánto** vas a tardar en llegar?* ("How long are you going to be?")
- *Mira la vista desde aquí. ¡**Qué** maravilla!* ("Look at the view from here. How wonderful!")

Relative pronouns

They have more than one function: they point out other people who have been mentioned before, and they introduce subordinate sentences. Let's see them in the following chart.

	Singular	Plural
Neuter	que, quien	quienes
Femenine	la que, la cual, cuanta, cuya	las que, las cuales, cuantas, cuyas
Masculine	el que, lo que, el cual, lo cual, cuanto, cuyo	los que, los cuales, cuantos, cuyos

For example:

- *Mara, **que** siempre anda a las corridas, salió sin desayunar.* ("Mary, who is always rushing, left without having breakfast.")

- *José, **quien** era el médico de turno, me atendió muy bien* ("José, who was the doctor in charge, took good care of me.")
- *El sillón tenía varias manchas, **las cuales** pudimos limpiar* ("The sofa had several stains, which we were able to remove.")

Exercises

1. Go back to the short story at the beginning of the chapter and write down all the pronouns you find.
2. Decide whether the following statements are true or false. Correct the false ones.
    a. Pronouns are the words we use to replace adjectives or adverbs in a sentence.
    b. Pronouns reflect gender and number.
    c. Pronouns are not used as antecedents.
3. In each sentence, you have the information you need to choose the correct personal pronoun:
    a. ...... vamos a partir temprano porque estamos cansadas. (1ra persona, plural, femenino, en posición sujeto)
    b. Mi hermano ganó un premio. Se ...... dieron en una ceremonia de entrega de diplomas. (3ra persona, singular, masculino, en posición objeto directo)
    c. A ...... no se los conté, pero he cambiado de trabajo. (2da persona, plural, femenino, en posición preposicional)
    d. Organizó esta fiesta para ...... (1ra persona, singular, masculino, en posición preposicional)
4. Choose the correct possessive pronoun:
    a. ¿Estas manzanas son suyas/tuyo?
    b. Tenemos que decidir si vamos en vuestro auto o en el nuestra/nuestro.
    c. Mi esposa se compró lentes porque se olvidó la suya/los suyos en casa.

    d. Encontré una lapicera en casa que estoy segura de que no es mía/tuya.
5. Write one sentence using each of the following pronouns:
    a. cuanta
    b. ninguno
    c. bastante
    d. tercio

Now that we've finished covering all the types of pronouns, you can go back to the start of the chapter and cross out everything you've learned from the list!

Chapter 5: Mastering Adjectives and Adverbs

Short Story: El pretendiente

El día está **soleado**. Hace calor. Por eso, Rebeca y Miriam buscan la **sombra** de los árboles para su **caminata**. Es el único lugar del club donde pueden **pasear** cómodamente. El único sin aire acondicionado, por lo menos.

—¿Qué me dices del hijo de Susana? —pregunta Rebeca.

—¿Daniel? —dice Miriam—. Me pareció un hombre **encantador**. Es médico, ¿sabías?

—Kinesiólogo, Miriam —dice Rebeca, **con tono aleccionador**—. Es kinesiólogo. No es lo mismo. Pero sí, un hombre encantador... aunque un poco **charlatán**, ¿no lo crees?

—No lo sé, Rebeca —contesta Miriam—. Es cierto que hablaba muy rápido... O muy bajo. Digamos que yo no le entendía bien. Pero eso me pasa con todas las personas jóvenes.

—Quizás deberías hacerte un **estudio de audición** —dice Rebeca—. Ya estamos en edad...

—Es cierto —contesta Miriam—. De hecho, quizás Daniel conoce a alguien. Le preguntaré. Además, es una buena excusa para conseguir su teléfono. Quiero **presentárselo** a mi hija.

—¿A Elisa? —pregunta Rebeca—. ¿Por qué? Ella es una muchacha tan hermosa, tan vital. ¿Tú crees que es un buen **pretendiente**?

—Es mejor candidato que **el anterior** —dice Miriam—. Ese hombre era increíblemente aburrido. Y me lo habías recomendado tú.

—Yo no sabía que Samuel era así —contesta Rebeca—. Parecía muy amable.

—Era muy amable, y **más aburrido que chupar un clavo** —dice Miriam **contundentemente**—. En cambio, Daniel es gracioso.

—Es cierto, no lo puedo negar —responde Rebeca—. Pero, ¿no crees que es un poco bajo?

—¿Bajo? —pregunta Miriam—. ¡Pero si mide más de un metro ochenta!

—¿En serio? —responde Rebeca—. A mí me pareció **bajito**. Quizás es por la forma de su cabeza. Tiene la cabeza muy grande. Eso lo hace parecer más pequeño.

—No sé si tiene la cabeza grande —contesta Miriam—. Pero la tiene bien ordenada. Es muy **buen mozo**. Yo creo que a Elisa le gustará.

—Si tú lo crees... —dice Rebeca, **derrotada.**

—Eso sí: es una lástima que Daniel esté casado —contesta Miriam—. Pero bueno, nadie es perfecto.

Vocabulary List

Spanish	English
soleado, soleada	sunny
la sombra	shade
la caminata	stroll
pasear	go for a walk

encantador, encantadora	charming
con tono aleccionador	like teaching a lesson
charlatán, charlatana	chatterbox
el estudio de audición	hearing test
presentar	introduce
pretendiente	suitor
el, la anterior	the previous one
más aburrido que chupar un clavo	like watching paint dry
contundentemente	bluntly
bajito, bajita	a little short
buen mozo	handsome
derrotada, derrotado	defeated

Grammar Section

As an intermediate student, you probably know that adjectives are the words we use to describe nouns and, in turn, that adverbs are the words we use to describe adjectives and adverbs. So, in this chapter, we'll go a bit deeper into these two important types of words, and we'll cover the following topics:

- adjectives used as nouns and adverbs
- the position of adjectives and adverbs
- comparison of adjectives and adverbs

- irregular comparatives
- idioms and sayings that use adjectives

Adjectives used as nouns and adverbs

Typically, adjectives are used to describe nouns. However, they have other functions. For example, adjectives can be used **as** nouns to refer to a person or thing that has the characteristic of the adjective. This characteristic identifies the noun and distinguishes it from the rest. As a general rule, we put an article before the adjective to make it a noun. It sounds a bit complicated, but it's really simple. Let's check some examples:

- *De todos los coches, **el rojo** es el que más me gusta* ("Out of all the cars, the red one is my favorite.")
- ***El alto** es el mejor jugador del equipo* ("The tall one is the best player on the team.")

Some adjectives can also work as adverbs. To do so, they have to be in their masculine singular form. Their function is to complement the verb, to tell us how the action is done. Let's see some examples:

- *Los equipos rivales jugaron **sucio*** ("The opposing teams played dirty.")
- *La comida olía **feo*** ("The food smelled bad.")

Let's look at those same word functioning as adjectives to see the difference:

- *Los **sucios** rivales ganaron con trampa* ("The dirty opponents won by cheating.")
- *La comida de ese lugar es **fea*** ("The food in that place is bad.")

The position of the adjective

Syntax is how a language arranges words to create sentences. If we are talking about adjectives and nouns, we can say that English and Spanish have a syntactical difference. In Spanish, as a general rule, the adjective should always be placed after the noun it's modifying. And as we can see in the example below, English does the opposite thing:

- *Siéntate en la silla **roja*** ("Sit in the red chair.")

However, as with any rule, there are some exceptions, some cases in which the adjective is placed before the noun. Let's take a look at them:

Demonstrative (*ese, este, aquel*) and possessive (*tu, mi, su, nuestro*) adjectives come before the nouns they describe. For example:

- ***Ese*** *coche no anda* ("That car doesn't work.")
- ***Mi*** *hermana vive lejos* ("My sister lives far away.")

Limiting adjectives, the ones that define number, quantity or amount, always come before the noun:

- *Vimos **diez** cóndores* ("We saw ten condors.")
- *Pasó **mucho** tiempo* ("A lot of time has passed.")

Adjectives that don't describe nor give new information, but put emphasis in an essential quality of the noun, tend to go before it:

- *La **fría** nieve caía sin parar* ("The cold snow came down nonstop.")
- *Probó la **dulce** miel* ("She tried the sweet honey.")

If we take the first example, we can say that being cold is an essential quality of snow, so the adjective does not add any new information; it just emphasizes this characteristic.

In the last exception, we can group the adjectives that present a change in meaning when we change their position:

- *El **pobre** hombre perdió a su familia en un accidente* ("The unfortunate man lost his family in an accident.")
- *El hombre **pobre** mendigaba en la calle* ("The indigent man begged in the street.")
- *Llegaron el **mismo** día que nosotros* ("They arrived on the same day as us.")
- *Quiere todo para ella **misma*** ("She wants everything for herself.")

It is common to see that these adjectives, which vary in meaning depending on their position in relation to the noun, usually have a valuative, subjective meaning when they are placed before the noun, and a determinative, objective meaning when they are placed after it. Some illustrative examples of such cases are the following:

- *Es una profesional, pero tiene **verdaderos** problemas para controlar su genio* ("She is a professional, but has serious problems controlling her temper.")
- *Esta película está basada en una historia **verdadera*** ("This film is based on a true story.")
- *Bastó un **simple** trámite para poner en marcha la obra municipal* ("A single paperwork was enough to get the municipal work underway.")
- *Era un examen muy **simple**, no voy a suspender* ("It was a very easy exam, I am not going to fail.")

The position of the adverb

The adverb moves more freely in the sentence. Its position will depend on what you want to emphasize. However, there are certain guidelines that we must know and follow, so let's check them out.

For the most part, adverbs are placed after the verb. This rule applies especially to adverbs of quantity and manner. Let's look at an example:

- *Me divierto **mucho** con mis amigas* ("I have a lot of fun with my friends.")

In compound tenses, the adverb cannot be placed between the auxiliary and the main verbs, as it happens in English. Let's see it below:

- **Siempre** te he escuchado; or
- Te he escuchado **siempre**; but not
- ✗ Te he **siempre** escuchado ("I've always listened to you.")

When adverbs modify an adjective or another adverb, they are placed before that adjective or adverb. For example:

- *No sabía **muy** bien qué quería, así que pidió una recomendación* (She didn't know exactly what she wanted, so she asked for a recommendation.)

Many adverbs of mode, place, or time can be placed at the beginning of a sentence or after the verb, like in these examples:

- ***Realmente** habían hecho un buen trabajo*; or
- *Habían hecho **realmente** un buen trabajo* ("They had done a really good job.")

Time adverbs are very versatile: they can be at the beginning of the sentence, after the verb, or at the end of the sentence:

- ***Mañana** llega tu hermano*; or
- *Llega **mañana** tu hermano*; or
- *Tu hermano llega **mañana*** ("Your brother arrives tomorrow.")

Comparison of adjectives and adverbs

To indicate that something is superior to something else, we use the following formula:

- *más + adjetivo/adverbio + que* (more + adjective/adverb + than or adjective/adverb + -er + than)

We have an example of this in the short story; have you noticed it?

- ***más aburrido que** chupar un clavo* (the literal translation would be "more boring than sucking on a nail")

Another example:

- *Luis está **más dormido que** yo* ("Luis is sleeper than me.")

If we want to indicate inferiority, we use a similar formula:

- *menos + adjetivo/adverbio + que* (less + adjective/adverb + than)

    For example:

- *El libro me pareció **menos entretenido que** la película* ("I found the book less entertaining than the movie.")

Lastly, to indicate that two things are equal using adjectives or adverbs, we use this construction:

- *tan + adjetivo/adverbio + como* or *igual de adjetivo/adverbio que* (as adjective/adverb + as)

For example:

- *Mi hijo es **tan lindo como** su padre* ("My son is as handsome as his father.")

Superlatives

Superlatives are used to say which noun (in a group of three or more) is "the most" or "the least." To do so, we use a very similar construction to the one used for comparatives. The only difference is that we add a definite article:

- *el/la/los/las + más + adjetivo* (the + most + adjective)
- *el/la/los/las + menos + adjetivo* (the + least + adjective)

For example:

- *Mi hija es **la más perfecta** de todos* ("My daughter is the most perfect girl of all.")
- *Estas son **las menos dulces*** ("These are the least sweet.")

Irregular comparatives

There are a few adjectives in Spanish that don't follow the rules we've just mentioned. We are talking about the irregular comparatives. I know the word "irregular" might frighten you, but don't worry, the list of irregular comparatives is short. Let's check it out:

Adjective	Comparative	Superlative
bueno	mejor	la/el mejor
malo	peor	la/el peor
grande	mayor	la/el mayor
pequeño	menor	la/el menor

One last thing worth noting about irregular comparatives is that *menor* and *mayor* are used for age. When we are talking about size, *grande* and *pequeño* follow the normal rules:

- *Esta es la casa más grande del vecindario* ("This is the biggest house in the neighborhood.")

Idioms and sayings with adjectives

To finish off this chapter, let's have some fun! Do you know any Spanish sayings? Do you want to learn some? We've made a list of the most common Spanish idioms that have adjectives in them for you to read and learn! Let's check it out:

Spanish	English
Estar más fresco que una lechuga.	Being as fresh as a daisy.
Ser más aburrido que una ostra.	Being as boring as watching paint dry.
Ser más viejo que Matusalén.	Being older than dirt.
Estar más contento que un perro con dos colas.	Being as happy as a clam.
Quedarse frito.	To fall asleep.
A caballo regalado no se le miran los dientes.	Don't look a gift horse in the mouth.
A ojo de buen cubero.	At a guess.
Andar de capa caída.	Being in low spirits.
Año nuevo, vida nueva.	New year, new life.
Blanco y en botella, leche.	If it looks like a duck and walks like a duck, it is a duck.
Quedarse con la boca abierta.	Be left with one's mouth open.
Pasar la noche en blanco.	To not sleep a wink.
Sacar los trapos sucios.	Don't wash your dirty linen in public.

Pagar los platos rotos.	To pay the piper.
Más vale tarde que nunca.	Better late than never.
Quien mucho abarca, poco aprieta.	Jack of all trades, master of none.
En menos de lo que canta un gallo.	In a jiffy.
Echar más leña al fuego.	To add fuel to the flames.
Al mal tiempo, buena cara.	If life gives you lemons, make lemonade.

Now that you have deepened your knowledge of the uses of adjectives and adverbs, let's test you!

Exercises

1. Use the definition between brackets to complete the following sentences with an adjective. What type of word is the adjective replacing?

    e. Mis perros están comiendo ...... (cantidad o intensidad escasos respecto de lo regular), lo que me tiene preocupada.

    f. Había tres mozos trabajando en el restaurante. A nosotros nos atendió el ...... (de gran estatura).

    g. Las palomas son aves de ciudad que suelen volar ...... (de poca altura).

    h. María se compró un auto nuevo. Había de muchos colores, pero se decidió por 61

2. Decide whether the following statements are true or false. Correct the false ones.

    a. Syntax is the way in which languages put in order the different types of words to create sentences that make sense.

b. In Spanish, the adjective is always placed after the noun it's modifying.

c. Demonstrative and possessive adjectives are placed after the noun.

d. *Nuevo* belongs to the group of adjectives that present a change in meaning depending on their position.

3. Decide whether the adjective in brackets should go before or after the noun:

   a. Mi ...... problema ...... es que no me gusta mi trabajo. (único)

   b. Le hicimos un ...... regalo ......: una primera edición de su libro preferido. (único)

   c. Mi hermano y yo somos ...... personas ......, pero igual nos llevamos muy bien. (diferentes)

   d. Antes de entrar a la universidad, deben rendir ...... exámenes ...... para corroborar el nivel. (diferentes)

4. Follow the example to provide the formula and an example to indicate:

   a. Superiority: *"más + adjetivo/adverbio + que": Corro más rápido que mis rivales.*

   b. Inferiority:

   c. Equality:

   d. Positive superlative:

   e. Negative superlative:

5. Match the common saying on the left with their meanings on the right:

a. Andar de capa caída. • Significa lo mismo que "pagar las consecuencias".

b. Quedarse frito.

c. Pagar los platos rotos. • Se usa para decir que una persona está triste.

d. Sacar los trapos sucios • Se usa para decir que se está hablando de cosas privadas en público.

- Significa lo mismo que quedarse dormido.

Chapter 6: Demonstrating How Articles Work

Short Story: El viaje

La **maleta** es más pequeña de lo que recordaba. No hay forma de que allí entre todo lo que quiere llevar.

"Una vida no **cabe** en una maleta como esta", piensa María. "Aunque, en realidad, una vida no cabe en ninguna maleta".

A pesar de todo, intenta otra vez guardar su ropa allí. Toma las **playeras** y las vuelve a doblar. Forma una bola con los **calcetines**. **Pliega** los **pantalones** hasta darles forma de cuadrado.

"Un **abrigo**", piensa María. "En Canadá hará frío".

María revisa su closet. Ve una **chaqueta de invierno**, un **sobretodo** y un **saco grueso**. Decide llevar la chaqueta, más **cálida**. Ya tendrá tiempo de comprar las demás prendas en Vancouver.

En ese momento, Jorge entra a la habitación.

—¿Cómo va eso? —pregunta Jorge.

María muestra sus manos llenas de ropa como respuesta. Jorge ríe y se acerca a ella. Comienza a doblar ropa. Es muy bueno en eso. Él siempre fue la persona más ordenada de la relación. Es meticuloso. Cuando salían de vacaciones, sus maletas siempre pesaban cinco kilos menos que las de María, pero jamás **echaba nada en falta**. Llevaba exactamente lo necesario.

—Pon unos **zapatos** extra —dice Jorge, mientras acomoda la ropa en la maleta—. **Por si se mojan** los que **llevas puestos**.

—No **entran** —responde María—. Ya lo intenté.

—Déjame a mí —dice Jorge.

Jorge saca la ropa de la maleta y la deja cuidadosamente sobre la cama. Después la vuelve a meter, pero en otro orden. Pone primero las playeras, los suéteres y los pantalones, más geométricos. Cuando está seguro de que todo el espacio está ocupado, empieza a colocar las prendas con forma más irregular: los calcetines, la ropa interior y la chaqueta de invierno. De pronto, la maleta parece más **espaciosa**. Antes de meter los zapatos, Jorge los rellena de calcetines, para no dejar ese espacio desocupado.

—Gracias —dice María finalmente—. Jorge, estoy **asustada**.

—¿Por qué? —pregunta Jorge—. Vancouver es una gran oportunidad. Es el trabajo que siempre soñaste.

—Sí, lo sé, pero... —contesta María—. Cuando soñaba con ese trabajo, no esperaba estar sola en una ciudad **helada**.

—Te las **arreglarás** —dice Jorge.

—Te voy a extrañar —responde María.

Jorge no responde. En cambio, busca en los cajones de la habitación compartida y saca una bufanda azul.

—Toma, no quiero que **pases frío** —dice Jorge, mientras se la pasa por el cuello a María.

Vocabulary List

Spanish	English
la maleta	suitcase
caber	fit
a pesar de todo	despite everything
la playera	t-shirt

los calcetines	socks
plegar	fold
los pantalones	trousers
el abrigo	coat
la chaqueta de invierno	winter jacket
el sobretodo	overcoat
el saco	jacket
grueso, gruesa	thick
cálido, cálida	warm
echar en falta	miss
los zapatos	shoes
por si	in case
mojarse	get wet
llevar puesto, puesta	be wearing
entrar	fit
espacioso, espaciosa	spacious
asustado, asustada	scared

helado, helada	freezing
arreglárselas	manage
pasar frío	be cold

Grammar Section

This is going to be a short chapter in which we'll deal with only two types of words:

- definite articles, and
- indefinite articles.

However, despite being short, functional words, they are critical. So, let's get to them!

In English and Spanish, nouns are often preceded by a definite or indefinite article. But, while English uses only "the," in Spanish, we choose from the four variations of the definite article, depending on the gender and number of the noun that comes after it.

The same happens with the indefinite article. English has "a," "an," and "some," whereas Spanish has four indefinite articles that change according to the gender and number of the noun.

And that's not all, because Spanish also has neuter article *lo*. This article, which doesn't carry gender, is used before adjectives to transform them into abstract nouns. For example, *Lo ideal sería que llegaras temprano* ("The ideal thing would be for you to arrive early.")

Take a look at this table with definite, indefinite, and neuter articles:

| | Masculine || Feminine ||
	Singular	Plural	Singular	Plural
Definite	el	los	la	las
Indefinite	un	unos	una	unas
Neuter	lo			

Definite and indefinite articles are some of the most used words in the Spanish language, so it's essential to learn to use them correctly. Definite articles are used to talk about concrete things that are known to the people involved in the conversation. Indefinite articles are used when one of the people involved in the conversation doesn't know precisely the noun being discussed. Let's take a more detailed look at the different uses of these articles.

Uses of the definite article:

1. To talk about people or things that are unique, of which there is not more than one.

- *El padre de Rita* ("Rita's father.")

Most people have only one father, so we are talking of a specific person.

2. To refer to a specific thing or person that we know.

- *La médica de mi familia atiende los martes* ("My family's doctor works on Tuesdays.")

We are talking about a specific doctor we know, not just any doctor.

3. To talk about things or people in general.

- *Los caribeños son alegres* ("Caribbeans are lively people.")

We are talking generally about all Caribbeans.

4. To talk about the time.

- *Son las cinco de la tarde* ("It's five o'clock in the afternoon.")
- *Quedamos a las dos* ("Let's meet at two.")

5. To talk about dates. Remember that, like in English, months don't take an article.

- *El 24 de mayo es mi cumpleaños* ("May 24th is my birthday.")
- *En agosto, empieza un trabajo nuevo* ("In August, she starts a new job.")

6. For parts of the day (morning, afternoon and evening).

- *Por la tarde iré a la farmacia* ("In the afternoon, I'll go to the chemist.")

7. To discuss quantities or frequencies with days, weeks, or months.

- *Me ducho una vez al día* ("I shower once a day.")
- Trabajo veinte días al mes ("I work twenty days a month.")

Uses of the indefinite article:

1. To talk about something or someone that is not concrete, that we don't know or that is part of a larger group.

- *Estoy buscando una médica de cabecera nueva* ("I'm looking for a new family doctor.")

We are talking about any doctor, one we don't know yet.

2. To talk about quantities in the singular and the plural.

- *Compré unos zapatos nuevos* ("I bought some new shoes.")
- *Tengo un auto* ("I have a car.")

Common mistakes

Now, let's talk about the most common mistakes Spanish students make with definite and indefinite articles.

- Using the definite article when you have to use the indefinite one, and vice versa
- Not using the articles when it's needed
- Using the article where it's not needed

- Using the definite or indefinite articles instead of the possessive

Let's pay attention to these two sentences to see how important it is to use them correctly:

- *Pregúntale a la maestra* ("Ask the teacher.")
- *Pregúntale a una maestra* ("Ask a teacher.")

Is there a difference between the two sentences? All we've done is change the definite article for an indefinite one. If we say *Pregúntale a una maestra*, we are telling you to go ask any teacher, the one you like the most. But if we say *Pregúntale a la maestra*, we are talking about a teacher that we both know - someone we've mentioned before.

Let's look at one last example.

- *Voy a comprar un ordenador* ("I am buying a computer.")
- *Voy a comprar el ordenador* ("I am buying the computer.")

What's the difference here? Again, the only difference between these two sentences is the articles, but those little words completely change the meaning. When we say *Voy a comprar un ordenador*, it means that we haven't yet chosen which computer we want; we just know that we are getting one. If we say *Voy a comprar el ordenador*, it means that we have already seen several computers and chosen one. We've already talked about which computer I liked, and we both know about it.

So, in sum, we can say that we use the definite article when the person who speaks and the person who listens know exactly the object being spoken about. And we use the indefinite article when the person speaking or the person listening doesn't exactly know the object being spoken about.

Exercises

1. Go back to the short story at the beginning of the chapter and underline all the articles you can find. Remember that these words can have other functions, like pronouns or adjectives. So, pay attention and only select the ones that are working as articles.

2. Decide whether the following statements are true or false. Correct the false ones.
   a. To choose the correct article, we have to consider the gender and number of the noun that comes after it.
   b. *Lo* is a masculine article.
   c. *Lo* is used in front of adjectives to transform them into abstract nouns.
   d. Definite articles are used to talk about things that are not known to the people involved in the conversation.

3. Rewrite the following sentences changing the nouns into abstract nouns made of adjectives like in the example
   a. La belleza de la vida es compartirla con los seres queridos: *Lo bello de la vida es compartirla con los seres queridos.*
   b. María se desesperó ante la dificultad del problema.
   c. Debieron cancelar la excursión por la frialdad del día.
   d. La simpleza de la vida en el campo resulta muy atractiva.

4. Complete the following short story with the corresponding articles.

   José y Luz están de vacaciones en Francia con ... pareja amiga, Miguel y Ana. A Miguel le encanta visitar edificios históricos, y José accede a acompañarlo a visitar algunos. Mientras, Luz y Ana deciden ir a conocer ... bar famoso. Caminando por ... pueblo, José y Miguel ven ... hermosa iglesia antigua. Sin embargo, cuando entran, hay ... servicio en marcha.

   —¡Shh! Quedémonos sentados en silencio para no llamar ... atención. Actuemos como ... demás —susurra Miguel.

   Como no saben francés, José y Miguel se sientan en silencio y observan ... iglesia. Durante ... servicio, se ponen de pie, se arrodillan y se sientan imitando lo que hace ... resto de ... asistentes.

   —¡Espero que no estemos llamando ... atención! —le dice

Miguel a José.

En un momento, ... cura dice algo, y ... hombre sentado delante de ellos se pone de pie.

Siguiendo su ejemplo, Miguel y José también se ponen de pie. De pronto, todos ... asistentes comienzan a reír.

Al finalizar ... servicio, ... cura se acerca a ... dos hombres y los saluda en español.

—¿Por qué todos se rieron? —pregunta José.

—Bueno, muchachos, ayer hubo ... nacimiento, y le pedí al padre que se pusiera de pie para felicitarlo.

5. Now, write a short story or narrate an anecdote in 150 words.

Awesome! After finishing the quiz, you can go back to the beginning and cross off everything you've learned from the list!

Mid-Book Quiz

¡Felicitaciones! You've reached the middle of the book. It's been quite a journey, hasn't it? But we are sure you have been learning a lot of Spanish while having a bit of fun. Now, it's time to test you on everything we've seen so far.

In this quiz, each correct answer is worth 2 points. If you get between 15 and 20 points, you're doing great! If you score between 10 and 15 points, you too are doing very well, but you are still in the middle of the learning process; we encourage you to go back and reread the sections on the questions you got wrong. If you get less than 10 points, don't worry! There's no rush. Take your time to go back to the beginning of the book and review everything. Once you've done that, you can retake the quiz. We are sure you'll do great the second time!

1. Resolve the following sums and write down the numbers in Spanish:
    a. 1.500 + 235:
    b. 10.000 + 9.583:
       And if we were talking about cows? How would you write those same numbers?
2. Can you write down two ways of asking for the time in Spanish?
   And now, answer the question with the following times:

a. 11:45 am

b. 4:10 pm

3. Are the following nouns masculine or feminine? Decide by choosing the correct article

   a. ... solución
   b. ... problema
   c. ... foto
   d. ... tortuga
   e. ... lumbre
   f. ... mano
   g. ... pie

4. What do we mean when we say that Spanish is a gendered language? What does "grammatical agreement" or "concord" mean?

5. What is the bolded pronoun replacing in each case?

   a. María llegó ayer a la noche. Todavía no **la** he visto.
   b. **Le** regalamos un rompecabezas a tu hermano. Hoy comenzó a armar**lo**.
   c. Estás enojado. **Eso** no te deja pensar con claridad.
   d. Mi madre nació en 1961 y mi padre en 1965, por lo que **ella** es mayor.

6. Complete with the corresponding demonstrative pronoun.

   a. ¿Me alcanzas ... cacerola? (object far from speaker and recipient)
   b. ¿Qué tal está ... tomate? (object close to recipient)
   c. Me gusta ... . ¿Sabes quién lo pintó? (object far from speaker and recipient)
   d. ... uvas que trajiste están buenísimas. (object close to speaker and recipient)

7. Where is the adjective typically placed in Spanish? Which types of adjectives are placed elsewhere?

8. Match the formula with the meaning:

   Superiority:
   Inferiority:
   Equality:
   Positive superlative

   "menos + adjetivo/adverbio + que"
   "más + adjetivo/adverbio + que"
   "el/la/los/las + más + adjetivo"
   "tan + adjetivo/adverbio + como"

9. Complete the following sentences with *definido* or *indefinido*:

   a. Para hablar de cantidades, usamos el artículo ......

   b. Usamos el artículo ...... para referirnos a cosas únicas, de las que no existe más de una.

   c. Para hablar de fechas y horas, usamos el artículo ......

   d. Cuando todas las personas involucradas en la conversación conocen de lo que se está hablando, usamos el artículo .... Por otro lado, usamos el artículo ...... cuando una de las personas de la conversación no conoce de lo que se está hablando.

10. Match the common saying in the left with their meanings in the right:

a. Blanco y en botella, leche.

- Se usa para decir que una persona que hace muchas cosas, no puede hacerlas todas bien.

b. Echar más leña al fuego.

- Significa medir algo de una forma imprecisa, sin ningún elemento de medición.

c. Quien mucho abarca, poco aprieta.

- Se usa cuando alguien está haciendo crecer un tema problemático.

d. A ojo de buen cubero.   • Se usa para decir que, si algo se parece a algo, probablemente lo sea.

Chapter 7: The Verb I. Focus on the Present

Short Story: ¿Quién es el más famoso?

Julio y Federico están sentados en una mesa del café de Paco. Ese es su lugar favorito. Paco siempre les **guarda** esa mesa. A partir de las tres de la tarde, nadie más que ellos puede sentarse allí. Y, desde hace veinte años, Julio y Federico la ocupan religiosamente.

En general, cuando se sientan en su mesa, Julio y Federico hacen dos cosas: beber café y discutir. El café siempre es el mismo, pero la discusión varía. A veces aprovechan los temas de actualidad. En esas ocasiones, uno de los dos **suele** tener un **periódico** en la mano, al que, al calor de la discusión, golpea y **agita sin piedad**.

Ese día, el tema de la discusión es otro. Julio y Federico debaten sobre cuál es el español más famoso del mundo. Han estado discutiendo ya por una hora. El **ambiente está caldeado**.

—¡Rafael Nadal! —exclama Federico—. ¿Lo dices en serio? ¿Quién será el próximo, Fernando Alonso?

—Nadal ha tenido una mejor carrera que Alonso —responde Julio.

—Si es por carreras, mejor ha sido la de Antonio Banderas —dice Federico.

—¡Antonio Banderas! —exclama Julio, indignado—. ¡Si la mitad del mundo cree que es mexicano! **Ni que fuera** Penélope Cruz. O Pedro Almodóvar.

—Nadie recuerda los nombres de los **directores de cine** —contesta Federico.

En ese momento, Paco, el **mozo** y dueño del café, interrumpe la discusión.

—Muchachos, bajen la voz —pide Paco—. Están **ahuyentando** a los clientes.

Julio y Federico miran a su alrededor. El café de Paco está casi vacío. Solo una de las mesas está ocupada por Herman, un hombre **rubio** de cara ancha.

—Aquí solo quedó Herman —dice Paco—. Quizás porque no habla muy bien español. Le resulta más fácil ignorarlos.

—Lo sentimos —agrega Julio.

—No se **preocupen**, no hay problema —responde Paco—. En realidad, sí hay problema. ¿Por qué ninguno habla de Picasso, o de Dalí?

—¡Dalí! —contesta Federico, otra vez **a los gritos**—. ¡No me hagas hablar de Dalí!

—Basta —dice Julio—. Terminemos con esto. Preguntémosle a Herman. Él es alemán. El primer español que nombre, es el más famoso. Y allí termina la discusión. Es casi como tirar una **moneda**. ¿Estamos de acuerdo?

—Vale —contesta Federico.

Entonces, Paco se **acerca** a la mesa de Herman, quien está mirando el móvil frente a su taza de café.

—Herman, disculpa —interrumpe Paco—. Quería hacerte una pregunta. ¿Quién es el español más famoso? El más famoso de todos.

Herman levanta la mirada del móvil. Responde sin dudar:

—Cervantes.

Vocabulary List

Spanish	English
guardar	keep
soler	usually do
el periódico	newspaper
agitar	shake
sin piedad	mercilessly
el ambiente caldeado	tense atmosphere
ni que fuera	not even if
el director de cine, la directora de cine	movie director
el mozo, la moza	waiter, waitress
ahuyentar	drive away
rubio, rubia	blond
preocuparse	worry
a los gritos	yelling, out loud
la moneda	coin
acercarse	get closer

Grammar Section

Verbs are often considered the most difficult part of a language to learn. But you don't need to worry. There is nothing to fear about a few conjugations. In this chapter, you will see that present tense verbs are not really difficult, and you will soon master:

- the present indicative
- the progressive or continuous present
- the present subjunctive

The present indicative

Since you are not new to the language, you probably already know that the present indicative tense in Spanish is similar to how it is used in English. The difficult part is that, in Spanish, the conjugations vary greatly depending on whether the verbs are regular or irregular.

In this section, we will start reviewing the regular verbs ending in -AR, -ER, and -IR and their conjugations. To conjugate a verb in the present indicative, you must drop the ending and then add the specific ending according to each pronoun.

Let's see three examples: *cantar* ("to sing"), *comer* ("to eat"), and *vivir* ("to live").

	cantar	**comer**	**vivir**
yo	canto	como	vivo
tú	cantas	comes	vives
él/ella	canta	come	vive
nosotros/nosotras	cantamos	comemos	vivimos
vosotros/vosotras	cantáis	coméis	vivís

| ellos/ellas | cantan | comen | viven |

When it comes to irregular verbs, things get a bit more difficult. Languages are often whimsical and follow particular rules. Therefore, don't worry if you can't correctly conjugate all the verbs below on the first try. Remember that practice makes perfect!

It's time to see some of the most used irregular verbs in Spanish and their conjugations in the present indicative. We will divide them into categories according to how the stem is modified.

Irregular verbs with vowel irregularities:

	contar ("to tell")	**perder** ("to lose")	**pensar** ("to think")
yo	cuento	pierdo	pienso
tú	cuentas	pierdes	piensas
él/ella	cuenta	pierde	piensa
nosotros/nosotras	contamos	perdemos	pensamos
vosotros/vosotras	contáis	perdéis	pensáis
ellos/ellas	cuentan	pierden	piensan

Irregular verbs with consonant irregularities:

	decir ("to say")	**hacer** ("to do")	**caer** ("to fall")
yo	digo	hago	caigo
tú	dices	haces	caes

él/ella	dice	hace	cae
nosotros/nosotras	decimos	hacemos	caemos
vosotros/vosotras	decís	hacéis	caéis
ellos/ellas	dicen	hacen	caen

Irregular verbs that completely change their stems:

	ser ("to be")	**ir** ("to go")
yo	soy	voy
tú	eres	vas
él/ella	es	va
nosotros/nosotras	somos	vamos
vosotros/vosotras	sois	vais
ellos/ellas	son	van

Uses of the present indicative

Now that we have reviewed the conjugations of the present indicative, let's refresh its uses. We use the present indicative to:

1. Talk about something specific that's happening at this very moment:

- *Quiero comer una hamburguesa* ("I want to eat a hamburger.")

2. Talk about frequent actions:

- *Héctor va a la escuela en autobús* ("Héctor goes to school by bus.")

3. Mention present desires:

- *Martín **piensa** en mudarse* ("Martín thinks about moving.")

4. Talk about situations that are going to happen in the near future:

- ***Tengo** una entrevista de trabajo el viernes* ("I have a job interview on Friday.")

5. Talk about things that are always true:

- *Los perros **ladran** y los gatos **maúllan*** ("Dogs bark and cats meow.")

6. Narrate events from the past:

- *La Primera Guerra Mundial **empieza** en 1914* ("World War I begins in 1914.")

The progressive present

The present progressive in Spanish, also known as "present continuous," is the tense we use to talk about something happening at the moment of speaking. It is also used to talk about actions that you are doing continuously for a certain period of time. Sounds familiar to you, right? You probably already studied this tense. And besides, English also has a present continuous: it's the tense formed by the verb "to be" plus a second verb followed by -ING, forming a gerund. "I sing" is in the simple present, and "I'm singing" is in the present continuous.

Now, let's review how to form the present continuous in Spanish. The formula is as follows:

The subject (it can be implicit) + **a reflexive pronoun** (*me, te, lo, nos*; if applicable) + **the verb *estar* conjugated** + **the stem of the main verb** + **the suffix -ANDO or -IENDO**

Take a look at three simple example sentences. Below them, you can see a table in which we will break down each sentence, so you can see the formula in detail:

- ***Estoy comiendo*** ("I am eating.")
- *El perro **está ladrando*** ("The dog is barking.")
- *Mis hermanas **se están peinando*** ("My sisters are combing their hair.")

Subject	Reflexive Pronoun	Conjugated Verb "estar"	Verb Stem	Suffix -ANDO or -IENDO
(Yo)		Estoy	com	iendo
El perro		está	ladr	ando
Mis hermanas	se	están	pein	ando

You might be wondering how to know when to use the suffix -ANDO and when to use the suffix -IENDO:

- Verbs ending in -AR: -ANDO. For example, *caminar* becomes *caminando* ("walking"), *mirar* becomes *mirando* ("looking"), and *cantar* becomes *cantando* ("singing").
- Verbs ending in -ER and -IR: -IENDO. For example: *escribir* becomes *escribiendo* ("writing"), *comer* becomes *comiendo* ("eating"), and *leer* becomes *leyendo* ("reading".)
  - Let's stop for a moment on the verb *leer*. As you have no doubt noticed, its gerund is not ✗ *leiendo*, but *leyendo*, with a Y. This happens with a few verbs, such as *ir* (*yendo*, "going"), *huir* (*huyendo*, "fleeing"), *caer* (*cayendo*, "falling"), and *creer* (*creyendo*, "believing").

Now, let's see a few example sentences with the present progressive:

- ***Estoy escribiendo*** *una novela* ("I am writing a novel.")
- *Parece que* ***estás disfrutando*** *de ese viaje* ("You seem to be enjoying that trip.")
- *Mariana* ***está viniendo*** *a mi casa* ("Mariana is coming to my house.")
- ***Estamos teniendo*** *algunos problemas con la conexión* ("We're having some problems with the connection.")

- *Os lo estáis pasando bien, ¿no?* ("You're having a great time, aren't you?")
- *Carlos y Walter se están convirtiendo en grandes amigos* ("Carlos and Walter are becoming great friends.")

The present subjunctive

The subjunctive is a verbal mood used to talk about hypothetical, possible or desired actions or situations. Verbs in the subjunctive mood are subordinate to another verb (which is in the indicative mood) within a sentence.

Forming present subjunctive in Spanish with regular verbs, the first step is to get their *root*. For example, the stem of *cantar* ("to sing") is *cant*, and the stem of *comer* ("to eat") is *com*. Then, you have to add the proper termination, depending on the case:

	Verbs ending in -AR	Verbs ending in -ER and in -IR
yo	-e	-a
tú	-es	-as
él/ella	-e	-a
nosotros/nosotras	-emos	-amos
vosotros/vosotras	-éis	-áis
ellos/ellas	-en	-an

Now, let's see the regular verbs *amar* ("to love"), *temer* ("to fear") and *partir* ("to leave") in the present subjunctive.

	amar	temer	partir
yo	ame	tema	parta
tú	ames	temas	partas
él/ella	ame	tema	parta
nosotros/nosotras	amemos	temamos	partamos
vosotros/vosotras	améis	temáis	partáis
ellos/ellas	amen	teman	partan

But what happens with irregular verbs? Once again, irregular verbs typically follow their own rules. Next, we will see the conjugation of the present subjunctive of some of the most used irregular verbs in Spanish.

	ser ("to be")	**decir** ("to say")	**ir** ("to go")
yo	sea	diga	vaya
tú	seas	digas	vayas
él/ella	sea	diga	vaya
nosotros/nosotras	seamos	digamos	vayamos
vosotros/vosotras	seáis	digáis	vayáis

| ellos/ellas | sean | digan | vayan |

Uses of the present subjunctive

We've already mentioned that the present subjunctive expresses hypothetical, possible, or desired actions or situations. However, there are some other uses, so let's see an example of each:

1. Expressing desire

- *Me gustaría que **llegaras** temprano* ("I would like for you to arrive early.")

2. Expressing necessity

- *Necesitamos que **repares** el coche para seguir el viaje* ("We need you to repair the car to continue with the trip.")

3. Expressing interests or feelings

- *Le encanta que le **regalen** flores* ("He loves to get flowers.")

4. Stating opinions or perceptions with a negative statement (check the difference between the two sentences below)

- *Creo que mañana **ceno** con mis padres* ("I think I'm having dinner with my parents tomorrow," *ceno* is in the indicative mood)
- *No creo que mañana **cene** con mis padres* ("I don't think I'm having dinner with my parents tomorrow," *cene* is in the subjunctive mood)

5. Expressing doubt and probability

- *Quizás **pueda** pasar mañana, pero no te lo prometo* ("I might be able to go tomorrow, but I'm not sure.")

6. Giving advice

- *Les recomiendo que **lleguen** temprano* ("I would advise you to arrive early.")

7. Giving orders

- *Mis padres me prohíben que **me acueste** muy tarde* ("My parents won't let me go to bed too late.")

8. Asking people to do something

- *Mi madre me pidió que **pase** por el supermercado* ("My mother asked me to go to the supermarket.")

9. Expressing purpose
- *Te regalamos la computadora para que **trabajes*** ("We gave you the computer so that you would work.")

10. Besides the uses listed above, there are some words and expressions that trigger the subjunctive:

Spanish	English
a no ser que	unless
a pesar de que	even though
antes de que	before
aunque	even if
con tal de que	as long as
cuando	when
después de que	after
en el caso de que	in case of
hasta que	until
sin que	without
tan pronto como	as soon as

Let's see some example sentences of present subjunctive in action:
- *Verónica siempre me pide que **sea** optimista* ("Verónica always asks me to be optimistic.")
- *Ojalá **apruebes** ese examen* ("I hope you pass that exam.")

- *Me alegra que **tengas** muchos amigos* ("I'm glad you have many friends.")
- *No creo que **llueva** mañana* ("I don't think it will rain tomorrow.")
- *¿Crees que Francisco **deba** estudiar mucho para ese examen?* ("Do you think Francisco should study hard for that exam?")
- *Mi vecino Pedro no siente que **esté** preparado para ese trabajo* ("My neighbor Pedro doesn't feel he is prepared for that job.")
- *Mi mamá dice que **vayamos** a comer* ("My mom says we should go eat.")
- *Espero que **tengáis** ganas de ir al parque* ("I hope you feel like going to the park.")
- *Quiero que mis hijos **lean** más* ("I want my children to read more.")

Are you ready to see how much you've learned in this chapter? Take the quiz and, afterward, go back and see if you can tick all the boxes!

Exercises

1. Miguel de Cervantes Saavedra is the most famous Spanish person, according to the German client in the bar in the short story at the beginning of this chapter. Complete the following text with the present indicative conjugations of the verbs, *llevar, pensar, haber, situar,* and, *ser* and *estar*.

    Cervantes .... considerado uno de los hombres más famosos de España. Muchos .... que su obra más importante, El Quijote, es una de las mejores de la literatura universal. El Museo Cervantes .... en Madrid, España, en la casa en la que se cree que nació el autor. Sin embargo, algunos .... su casa de nacimiento a unos minutos a pie, donde hoy .... un teatro que .... su nombre.

2. In the first column, you have some verbs, accompanied by their roots. In the right column, you have the endings of those verbs in the present indicative. Match the items on the

left with the items on the right to form the correct conjugations.

tener (ten-)   -emos

estar (est-)   -omos

decir (dec-)   -amos

hacer (hac-)   -imos

ser (s-)   -emos

3. In the next dialogue, complete the empty spaces with the present progressive. You have to use the verbs *construir*, *tener*, *ir* and *hacer*.
A. ¿*Cómo te .... en tu nuevo emprendimiento? Me dijo Julieta que .... muchos clientes.*
B. *Sí. Mudarnos al centro de la ciudad fue una gran decisión. El único problema es que .... un edificio al lado de la tienda. ¡El ruido de las máquinas se nos .... insoportable!*

4. Here you have some verbs. Below them, there are four possible options to form their gerund. Underline the correct one.

Ser	Comer	Hacer	Bailar
siendo	*comando*	*haciando*	*bailendo*
siando	*comiando*	*haciendo*	*balando*
sendo	*comiendo*	*hiciendo*	*bailondo*
siondo	*comiondo*	*haciondo*	*bailando*

5. Decide whether the following statements are true or false. Correct the false ones.
   a. The present indicative is used to talk about frequent actions.
   b. The present indicative can't be used to talk about the near future.
   c. The present progressive is used to talk about something that is happening at this very moment.
   d. The present subjunctive is used to talk about hypothetical, possible or desired actions or situations.

Chapter 8: The Verb II. Thinking About the Past

Short Story: La ciudad antigua

—Muy bien, aquí termina el tour por la Catedral de Sevilla —dijo Laura—. Si queréis, ahora podéis subir a la Giralda, que es esta torre de aquí. —Laura señaló la entrada a un edificio de **ladrillo** de unos noventa metros—. Como ya sabéis, originalmente no era parte de la Catedral. En realidad, la Giralda era parte de la mezquita de la ciudad, construida durante el siglo XII. Sigue siendo uno de los puntos más altos de Sevilla, así que os recomiendo subir. El único problema es que no tiene elevadores. Ahora sí: ¡adiós!

Los turistas aplaudieron para despedir a Laura. Ella les agradeció y después recogió los **auriculares** que les había entregado al principio del tour. Laura siempre estaba muy atenta a los auriculares. Una vez, hacía dos años, había perdido uno y había tenido que pagarlo con su propio dinero. No eran **baratos**.

Laura decidió tomarse su **recreo** para **almorzar**. Avisó a su **jefe** y salió de la Catedral, cruzando el Patio de los Naranjos. Estaban **en flor**. Cada vez que sentía el aroma a azahar de los **naranjos**, Laura agradecía mentalmente a Hércules, fundador mitológico de Sevilla, por traer la "manzana de oro" a España. Y agradecía también al califato almohade, que gobernó la ciudad durante el **medioevo**, porque había plantado naranjos en toda la ciudad.

La Plaza del Triunfo estaba **llena** de turistas. La primavera era siempre la **época** más **concurrida**. Laura caminó hasta **alejarse** de la **multitud**. Era imposible comer alrededor de esa plaza. Todo era muy caro.

Laura caminó hasta un pequeño bar a orillas del Guadalquivir. Le gustaba almorzar mirando el río. Por ese **mismo** río, pensaba, habían entrado todas las riquezas de América durante el siglo XVI. Había sido mucho tiempo atrás, pero su impacto **todavía** era notable. El Real Alcázar, a **apenas** unos metros, era un buen testimonio de eso.

—¿Qué quieres hoy, Laura? —preguntó Gonzalo, el **camarero**. Se conocían bien. Laura había visitado ese bar prácticamente todos los días durante dos años. Sabía que Gonzalo era fanático del Betis y que su madre había nacido en Venezuela.

— Salmorejo y chipirones, por favor —respondió Laura.

Gonzalo fue a la cocina, y Laura miró el río. Todavía le quedaban tres tours para esa tarde, pero eso no le preocupaba. Le gustaba su trabajo. Contar la historia de su ciudad le hacía sentir parte de algo más grande. Grande como el Guadalquivir. Algo que fluía, crecía, avanzaba, y que sin embargo era siempre parte de lo mismo.

Vocabulary List

Spanish	English
el ladrillo	brick
los auriculares	headphones
barato, barata	cheap
el recreo	break
almorzar	have lunch

el jefe, la jefa	boss
en flor	in bloom
el naranjo	orange tree
el medioevo	Middle Ages
lleno, llena	full
la época	time
concurrido, concurrida	crowded
mismo, misma	same
todavía	yet
apenas	barely
el camarero, la camarera	waiter, waitress

Grammar Section

We have already seen how to talk about the present. But you also need to know how to talk about the past. There are four past tenses in Spanish, and they are precisely the ones we are going to talk about in this chapter:

- *pretérito perfecto simple* (simple past);
- *pretérito perfecto* (perfect past)
- *pretérito imperfecto* (imperfect past); and
- *pretérito pluscuamperfecto*.

Don't let the names of those verb tenses scare you. We will go one by one, explaining the conjugations and giving you many examples. Let's go!

Pretérito perfecto simple

Let's start with the simplest of all. *Pretérito perfecto simple*, also known as *pasado simple* ("simple past") or *pretérito indefinido*, is used to talk about actions that happened at a specific time and have already been finished. This tense is usually accompanied by a time expression that specifies when that action took place, but it can also be implicit.

Pretérito perfecto simple is used to talk about:

1. Specific events that happened at a specific time:

- *El año pasado,* **cambié** *de trabajo* ("Last year, I changed jobs.")

2. Events that happened during a specific period of time.

- **Estuve** *más de dos horas esperando que me atendieran* ("I waited for more than two hours to be served.")

3. A new action that interrupts another.

- *Ayer estaba paseando y* **me encontré** *a mi hermana* ("Yesterday I was taking a walk and I ran into my sister.")

4. A sequence of actions that have already been finished.

- *Esta mañana,* **me desperté** *temprano,* **desayuné** *ligero y* **salí** *a dar una vuelta* ("This morning, I woke up early, I had a light breakfast and I went for a walk.")

Now that you know in what contexts you have to use the simple past in Spanish, let's see some example sentences.

- *Ayer* **vi** *una comadreja en el patio trasero* ("Yesterday I saw a weasel in the backyard.")
- *¿***Viajaste** *alguna vez al Caribe?* ("Have you ever been to the Caribbean?")
- *Rodrigó* **comió** *pizza, pero Rebeca* **pidió** *una hamburguesa* ("Rodrigo had pizza but Rebeca ordered a hamburger.")
- *Mis amigas y yo* **fuimos** *a la fiesta anoche* ("My friends and I went to the party last night.")
- *Vosotros* **tuvisteis** *mucha suerte* ("You were very lucky.")
- *Los gatos* **treparon** *al techo de la casa* ("The cats climbed to the roof of the house.")

Now let's see a table with the conjugations in *pretérito perfecto simple* of some common verbs in Spanish. Let's start with three regular verbs ending in -AR, -ER and -IR: *amar* ("to love"), *temer* ("to fear") and *partir* ("to leave").

	amar	temer	partir
yo	amé	temí	partí
tú	amaste	temiste	partiste
él/ella	amó	temió	partió
nosotros/nosotras	amamos	temimos	partimos
vosotros/vosotras	amasteis	temisteis	partisteis
ellos/ellas	amaron	temieron	partieron

Now, let's see the conjugations with four irregular verbs: *hacer* ("to do"), *ser* and *ir* ("to be" and "to go"; in this tense they have the same conjugation), and *andar* ("to walk" or "to be").

	hacer	ser/ir	andar
yo	hice	fui	anduve
tú	hiciste	fuiste	anduviste
él/ella	hizo	fue	anduvo
nosotros/nosotras	hicimos	fuimos	anduvimos

vosotros/vosotras	hicisteis	fuisteis	anduvisteis
ellos/ellas	hicieron	fueron	anduvieron

Pretérito perfecto

Pretérito perfecto, also known as *pasado compuesto* ("compound past"), is another verb tense used to talk about actions that took place in the past.

It's formed with the auxiliary verb *haber* ("to have") conjugated in *pretérito perfecto simple* (*he, has, ha, hemos, habéis, han*), followed by the verb that denotes the action conjugated in the *participio* ("participle"). But... what is the *participio?* Here you have some examples:

Verb	Participle
ser	sido
tener	tenido
saber	sabido
hacer	hecho
correr	corrido
amar	amado

In sum, the formula to conjugate a verb in *pretérito perfecto* is the following:

Subject + auxiliary verb *haber* (conjugated in *pretérito perfecto*) + participle of the main verb

This tense is used to:

1. Talk about past actions that have some link with the present:

- *He pensado en viajar a Perú a fin de año* ("I've been thinking about going to Peru at the end of the year.")

2. Talk about life experiences:

- *Ha visitado Francia en más de una ocasión* ("She's been to France more than once.")

Now, let's see some example sentences with the *pretérito perfecto*.

- *He visto una película muy buena en el cine* ("I've seen a very good movie in the theatre.")
- *¿Le has dado de comer a los perros?* ("Have you fed the dogs?")
- *Creo que tu teléfono se ha roto* ("I think your phone's broken.")
- *Nos hemos puesto muy contentos cuando llamasteis* ("We were very happy when you called.")
- *Habéis sabido manejar la situación muy bien* ("You managed to handle the situation perfectly.")
- *Esos mosquitos me han molestado toda la tarde* ("Those mosquitoes have been bothering me all afternoon.")

Now, we are going to see a table with common verb conjugations. We are going to use the same verbs ending in -AR, -ER and -IR that we used in the previous section.

	amar	temer	partir
yo	he amado	he temido	he partido
tú	has amado	has temido	has partido
él/ella	ha amado	ha temido	ha partido
nosotros/nosotras	hemos amado	hemos temido	hemos partido
vosotros/vosot	habéis amado	habéis temido	habéis partido

ras			
ellos/ellas	han amado	han temido	han partido

Now, let's see three irregular verbs: *hacer* ("to do"), *ser* ("to be"), and *ir* ("to go").

	hacer	ser	ir
yo	he hecho	he sido	he ido
tú	has hecho	has sido	has ido
él/ella	ha hecho	ha sido	ha ido
nosotros/nosotras	hemos hecho	hemos sido	hemos ido
vosotros/vosotras	habéis hecho	habéis sido	habéis ido
ellos/ellas	han hecho	han sido	han ido

Pretérito imperfecto

Pretérito imperfecto ("imperfect past") is a past tense used when the beginning or end of an action is not indicated. It is used to:

1. Talk about habitual or repeated actions in the past:

- *Cuando era una niña, **dibujaba** todo el día* ("When I was a little girl, I used to draw all day.")

2. Describe how an action took place in the past:

- *Los caballos **corrían** en el campo* ("The horses **were running** in the field.")

3. Point out an action in the past that is interrupted by a specific new action; the latter, expressed in *pretérito perfecto simple*:

- *Mientras **caminaba** por la playa, se acercó un amistoso perro* ("As he walked along the beach, he was approached by a friendly dog.")

4. Describe the state of a person or an object:

- *Martín **estaba** muy nervioso* ("Martín was very nervous.")

Let's see some example sentences with *pretérito imperfecto*:

- *¡Yo no sabía que me **estabais** organizando una fiesta sorpresa!* ("I didn't know you were organizing a surprise party for me!")
- *Recuerdo que **bailabas** tango muy bien* ("I remember that you danced tango very well.")
- *Teresa **trabajaba** en una inmobiliaria, pero le **pagaban** bastante mal* ("Teresa used to work in a real estate agency, but she was paid quite poorly.")
- *Mi madre y yo **pensábamos** que el vestido era más caro* ("My mother and I thought the dress was more expensive.")
- *¿Vosotros **veíais** esa serie cuando erais pequeños?* ("Did you watch that TV show when you were little?")
- *Mis tíos **vivían** en Sevilla* ("My aunt and uncle used to live in Seville.")

Pretérito imperfecto is formed with the stem of the verb followed by the corresponding ending according to each type of verb. Let's take a look at them.

Verbos terminados en -AR

yo		-aba
tú	raíz del verbo	-abas
él/ella		-aba
nosotros/nosotras		-ábamos

vosotros/vosotras		-abais
ellos/ellas		-aban

Examples:

	dar ("to give")	**bailar** ("to dance")	**soñar** ("to dream")
yo	daba	bailaba	soñaba
tú	dabas	bailabas	soñabas
él	daba	bailaba	soñaba
nosotros/nosotras	dábamos	bailábamos	soñábamos
vosotros/vosotras	dabais	bailabais	soñabais
ellos/ellas	daban	bailaban	soñaban

Verbos terminados en -ER y en -IR

yo		-ía
tú		-ías
él/ella	raíz del verbo	-ía
nosotros/nosotras		-íamos
vosotros/vosotras		-íais

ellos/ellas		-ían

Examples:

	beber ("to drink")	**comer** ("to eat")	**abrir** ("to open")
yo	bebía	comía	abría
tú	bebías	comías	abrías
él	bebía	comía	abría
nosotros/nosotras	bebíamos	comíamos	abríamos
vosotros/vosotras	bebíais	comíais	abríais
ellos/ellas	bebían	comían	abrían

Finally, we have three verbs that follow their own rules: *ser* ("to be"), *ir* ("to go"), and *ver* ("to see").

	ser	**ir**	**ver**
yo	era	iba	veía
tú	eras	ibas	veías
él	era	iba	veía
nosotros/nosotras	éramos	íbamos	veíamos
vosotros/vosot	erais	ibais	veíais

ras			
ellos/ellas	eran	iban	veían

Pretérito pluscuamperfecto

The final past tense we'll see in this book is *pretérito pluscuamperfecto*. It may sound complicated, but we assure you it's pretty simple: it is used to talk about the past of the past. Thus, you have to use it when talking about a past story and referring to something that happened before.

To conjugate *pretérito pluscuamperfecto*, you must take the auxiliary verb *haber* ("to have") in *pretérito imperfecto* followed by the *participio* of the main verb.

Let's see how to use *pretérito pluscuamperfecto* with some example verbs.

Subject	Auxiliary Verb (*haber*)	Participle of the Main Verb
yo	había	andado comido hecho bebido temido soñado
tú	habías	
él	había	
nosotros/nosotras	habíamos	
vosotros/vosotras	habíais	
ellos/ellas	habían	

Now, let's see the *pretérito pluscuamperfecto* in action with some example sentences:
- *Nunca antes **había caminado** por ese vecindario* ("I had never walked through this neighborhood.")

- *¿Ya **habías comido** paella alguna vez?* ("Had you had paella before?")
- *La profesora dijo que Rubén **había hecho** trampa en el examen* ("The professor said Rubén had cheated in the exam.")
- ***Habíamos pensado** vacacionar en Brasil, pero finalmente optamos por el sur de Argentina* ("We had thought about going on holiday to Brazil, but we ended up deciding to go to the south of Argentina.")
- *¿**Habíais pensado** alguna vez en casaros?* ("Had you ever thought about getting married?")
- *Cuando le llegó su turno, le dijeron que los boletos **se habían agotado*** ("When it was his turn, they told him that the tickets had sold out.")

Exercises

1. Below, you'll find a dialogue full of verbs in the past tense. Decide to which tense each one belongs (*pretérito perfecto simple, pretérito perfecto, pretérito imperfecto* or *pretérito pluscuamperfecto*).
A. Me **ha dicho** (..............) Cristina que eres ingeniero. Yo también **quería** (..............) estudiar esa carrera cuando era joven, pero finalmente me **decidí** (..............) por Medicina.
B. Sí, **estudié** (..............) Ingeniería, aunque al principio me **había anotado** para estudiar Arquitectura. ¡Pero me **arrepentí** (..............) en el último momento!

2. Decide whether the following statements are true or false. Correct the false ones.
    a. To form *pretérito perfecto* you need the participle of the verb.
    b. *Pretérito imperfecto* is the past tense that indicates the beginning or the end of an action.
    c. *Había hecho* is conjugated in *pretérito imperfecto*.
    d. *Pretérito perfecto simple* is used to talk about actions that occurred at a certain time but have already finished.

3. Complete the sentences with the correct ending of *pretérito imperfecto* (-ABA, -ABAS, -ÁBAMOS, -ABAIS, -ABAN).
   a. Mis amigos bail.......
   b. Juan cant.......
   c. Yo soñ.......
   d. Nosotros estudi.......
4. Go back to the short story at the beginning of the chapter and write down all the verbs conjugated in the *pretérito pluscuamperfecto* that you can find.
5. Complete the story below with the correct conjugated verbs. The verbs can be in any of the four past tenses we saw throughout the chapter.

María .... *(estar)* abriendo las persianas de su tienda, como todas las mañanas, cuando .... *(entrar)* un cliente nuevo. .... *(ser)* un hombre al que nunca .... *(ver)* antes, aunque algo en su cara le .... *(resultar)* familiar. .... *(tener)* un tupido bigote bajo la gran nariz.
—¡Buenos días! ¿En qué lo puedo ayudar? —.......... *(preguntar)* María.
—Quiero un café grande, por favor —.......... *(pedir)* el hombre, mientras .... *(jugar)* con su bigote.
María se .... *(dirigir)* hacia la cafetera y .... *(empezar)* a hacer el café. Mientras lo .... *(preparar)*, ... *(notar)* que la voz del hombre también le .... *(sonar)* conocida.
—Disculpe, ¿nos .... *(ver)* antes?
Entonces, con una sonrisa, el hombre se .... *(quitar)* el bigote de la cara. .... *(ser)* un bigote falso, por supuesto.
María .... *(dejar)* el café sobre el mostrador, incrédula.
—¿Eduardo? —.......... *(preguntar)*—. ¡Qué bonita sorpresa me .... *(dar)*!

Chapter 9: The Verb III. Towards the Future

Short Story: La feria del futuro

Manuel toma la mano de su madre. Tiene miedo de **perderse** entre la **multitud**. Nunca ha visto tanta gente junta en su vida.

Su madre le **señala** el cartel que decora el edificio donde van a entrar.

—Manuel, ¿qué dice allí? —pregunta.

Manuel mira detenidamente. En la escuela está aprendiendo a leer, pero todavía le **cuesta** hacerlo **de corrido**.

—Expo-sición Inter-na-cional —dice Manuel con dificultad— de Barcelona. 1929 —concluye, satisfecho.

Su madre sonríe y lo lleva al interior del edificio. Es uno de los muchos pabellones que construyeron en la ciudad para **albergar** la exposición. Manuel nunca ha estado en un lugar tan grande.

Caminan entre los distintos expositores. Su madre avanza despacio, porque no quiere perderse nada. Manuel escucha fragmentos de distintos **discursos**.

—En el futuro, cada familia tendrá un cine... ¡en su propia casa! —dice un hombre con **bigote**.

—¿Cansada de hacer la **colada**? —pregunta otro hombre a una mujer del público, mientras señala **una especie de** gran caja de metal—. Con esta maravillosa máquina, ¡no lavará una **prenda** más en su vida!

—Nadie tendría que **perder el tiempo** haciendo tediosas cuentas matemáticas —dice un tercer hombre, mientras **teclea** sobre algo que parece una **máquina de escribir**—. ¿Saben lo que Newton habría podido hacer con esta calculadora mecánica? ¡Maravillas!

Manuel piensa que a él también le vendría bien esa calculadora. La tarea de matemáticas sería mucho más sencilla.

Finalmente, su madre se detiene frente a un **puesto** de automóviles. Allí está el padre de Manuel, hablando frente a la multitud.

—Tres cosas son seguras —dice—. En el futuro, no hará falta trabajar. Trabajarán las máquinas. Además, ya no comeremos la porquería que comemos hoy. Habrá **pastillas** científicamente diseñadas para darnos fuerza y vigor. Y finalmente, por supuesto, los coches volarán por los aires. —En ese momento, el padre de Manuel señala al vehículo que tiene detrás—. Este modelo no vuela, pero está muy cerca.

Manuel mira el coche que su padre señala y recuerda todos los avances que vio en su **recorrido**. "El futuro será un lugar maravilloso", piensa. "No puedo esperar".

Vocabulary List

Spanish	English
perderse	get lost
la multitud	crowd
señalar	point at
costarle algo a alguien	find it hard

de corrido	fluently
albergar	be home to
el discurso	speech
el bigote	mustache
la colada	laundry
una especie de	a kind of
la prenda	item of clothing
perder el tiempo	waste time
teclear	type
la máquina de escribir	typewriter
el puesto	stand
la pastilla	pill
el recorrido	tour

Grammar Section

We've already talked about the past and the present. Now is the time to talk about the future! In this chapter we'll see the following future tenses:

- *futuro simple*;
- *futuro compuesto*;
- *condicional simple*; and

- *condicional compuesto.*

Futuro simple

In Spanish, *futuro simple* ("simple future") is used to:

1. Express the intention of doing an action in the future:

- *Mañana viajaré a Buenos Aires* ("Tomorrow I will travel to Buenos Aires.")

2. Express hypotheses or assumptions:

- *María se fue a pie; vivirá cerca* ("María left on foot; she probably lives nearby.")

Now, it's time to learn how to conjugate verbs in *futuro simple*. For verbs of the first, second, and third conjugation (verbs ending in -AR, -ER, and -IR, respectively), you have to include the stem of the verb followed by the corresponding ending, as we show in the chart below:

yo		-é
tú		-ás
él/ella	raíz del verbo	-á
nosotros/nosotras		-emos
vosotros/vosotras		-éis
ellos/ellas		-án

Let's see the conjugation in action with the verbs *amar, temer* and *partir*.

	amar	temer	partir
yo	amaré	temeré	partir
tú	amarás	temerás	partirás

él/ella	amará	temerá	partirá
nosotros/nosotras	amaremos	temeremos	partiremos
vosotros/vosotras	amaréis	temeréis	partiréis
ellos/ellas	amarán	temerán	partirán

And now let's check a few examples:
- *Partiré mañana a las ocho en punto* ("I will leave tomorrow at 8 o'clock.")
- *Carlos me dijo que vivirá en Bogotá un año* ("Carlos told me that he will live in Bogotá for a year.")
- *Te amaré por siempre* ("I will love you forever.")
- *Lucía cenará con sus amigas esta noche* ("Lucía will have dinner with her friends tonight.")

As we have seen in chapter 4 of this book, reflexive pronouns are used to indicate that an action falls on the subject. In this tense, the reflexive pronoun (*me, te, se, nos, os, se*) is always placed before the verb:
- *Me bañaré por la noche* ("I will shower tonight.")
- *Nos encontraremos a las siete* ("We will meet at 7.")
- *Te diré lo que pienso* ("I'll tell you what I think.")

When it comes to irregular verbs, the formula changes. We can divide them into three groups; let's look at them below.

Poner, salir, tener, venir, and valer

To conjugate these verbs in *futuro simple*, you must replace the E or the I of the infinitive by a D. Then, you have to add the corresponding ending according to the subject. Let's see a table with the conjugation of *poner, salir* and *tener*.

	poner	salir	tener
yo	pondré	saldré	tendré
tú	pondrás	saldrás	tendrás
él/ella	pondrá	saldrá	tendrá
nosotros/nosotras	pondremos	saldremos	tendremos
vosotros/vosotras	pondréis	saldréis	tendréis
ellos/ellas	pondrán	saldrán	tendrán

Let's see some examples:

- **Pondré** *el libro de quejas a disposición de los clientes* ("I will make the complaint book available to customers.")
- *Imagino que* **saldrás** *a almorzar pronto* ("I imagine you'll be out for lunch soon.")
- *Esto es una reliquia, ¡***valdrá*** mucho más en el futuro!* ("This is a relic, it will be worth much more in the future!")
- **Tendremos** *una noche magnífica junto a toda la familia* ("We will have a magnificent night with the whole family.")
- **Vendréis** *al pícnic en el parque, ¿verdad?* ("You're coming to the picnic in the park, right?")
- *Roberto y Paco* **saldrán** *a comer algo* ("Roberto and Paco are going out to have something to eat.")

Saber, querer, haber, poder, and caber

In this second group, the vowel ending of the infinitive (the E) disappears. For example, with *saber* we have to remove the E and we'll get *sabr-*. Then, we add the corresponding ending to this new stem. Let's see it in more detail:

	saber	querer	poder
yo	sabré	querré	podré
tú	sabrás	querrás	podrás
él/ella	sabrá	querrá	podrá
nosotros/nosotras	sabremos	querremos	podremos
vosotros/vosotras	sabréis	querréis	podréis
ellos/ellas	sabrán	querrán	podrán

For example:

- *No sé si **podré** hacer eso que me pides* ("I don't know if I can do what you're asking me.")
- *Supongo que **querrás** saber las razones de esta decisión* ("I guess you want to know the reasons for this decision.")
- *¿**Cabremos** todos en el mismo coche?* ("Will we all fit in the same car?")
- *Confiad en mí: **sabréis** qué hacer* ("Trust me: you'll know what to do.")
- *Me imagino que mis gatos **querrán** su alimento* ("I imagine my cats want their food.")

Hacer and decir

The third group is made up of the verbs *hacer* ("to do") and *decir* ("to say"). These two verbs change their stems and then take the ending of *futuro simple*. Let's see them in the table below.

	hacer	decir
yo	haré	diré
tú	harás	dirás
él/ella	hará	dirá
nosotros/nosotras	haremos	diremos
vosotros/vosotras	haréis	diréis
ellos/ellas	harán	dirán

For example:
- *Haré* las maletas por la tarde ("I'll pack in the afternoon.")
- ¿Le *dirás* a Martín la verdad? ("Will you tell Martín the truth?")
- Cristina *hará* su especialidad: ¡lasagna! ("Cristina will make her speciality: lasagna!")
- *Diremos* todo lo que pensamos al respecto ("We will say everything we think.")
- *Haréis* un gran espectáculo mañana ("You will put on a great show tomorrow.")
- Estoy ansiosa por saber qué *dirán* los críticos ("I'm anxious to know what the critics will say.")

Futuro compuesto

Futuro compuesto ("compound future", also known as *futuro perfecto*) is used to:

1. Talk about an action that will happen in the future, but will end before another future action:
- Ya *habré finalizado* mis estudios universitarios para el año que viene.

2. Express the assumption that an action happened in the past:

- *Juan aún no llega. ¿**Habrá tenido** algún problema?*

As you have undoubtedly noticed, the formula for *futuro compuesto* is quite simple: it's made up of the auxiliary verb *haber* in the *futuro simple*, followed by the *participio* of the main verb. Let's see how to form the *futuro compuesto* with some example verbs.

Subject	Auxiliary Verb (*haber*)	Participle of the Main Verb
yo	habré	andado comido hecho bebido temido soñado
tú	habrás	
él/ella	habrá	
nosotros/nosotras	habremos	
vosotros/vosotras	habréis	
ellos/ellas	habrán	

Now, let's see the *futuro compuesto* in action with some example sentences. Note how, when it expresses an action that will happen in the future, but will end before another future action, it is used together with some time adverb or some expression that refers to time.

- *Ya **habré cenado** para las nueve* ("I'll have had dinner by nine.")
- *¿El lunes **habrás vuelto**?* ("Will you be back by Monday?")
- *¡Está todo mojado! **Habrá llovido*** ("It's all wet! It has probably rained.")
- *Cuando nos demos cuenta, **habremos llegado*** ("When we realize it, we will have arrived.")
- *Mi casa no está por ese barrio. Os **habréis perdido*** ("My house isn't in that neighborhood. You're probably lost.")

- *Para mañana a esta hora, Juan y Teresa se **habrán casado*** ("By this time tomorrow, Juan and Teresa will have gotten married.")

Condicional simple

Condicional simple has many uses:

1. To express a desire:

- *Me **encantaría** adoptar un gatito* ("I would love to adopt a kitten.")

2. To make a polite invitation:

- *¿**Querrías** venir a casa mañana por la tarde?* ("Would you like to come to my house tomorrow afternoon?")

3. To ask for something politely:

- *¿**Podrías** llevarme en tu coche?* ("Could you take me in your car?")

4. To make a suggestion:

- *Lo mejor **sería** salir ahora, o llegaremos tarde* ("The best thing would be to leave now or we will be late.")

5. To express an assumption about the future by placing the starting point of the action in the past:

- *Bárbara dijo que **llegaría** tarde* ("Barbara said she would be late.")

Let's see how to conjugate in *condicional simple* the regular verbs ending in -AR, -ER, and -IR.

yo	verbo en infinitivo	-ía
tú		-ías
él/ella		-ía
nosotros/nosotras		-íamos
vosotros/vosotras		-íais
ellos/ellas		-ían

Condicional compuesto

Condicional compuesto is made up of the verb *haber* as an auxiliary, followed by the participle of the main verb. In this tense, *haber* is conjugated in the conditional. The *condicional compuesto* is used to:

1. Talk about hypothetical possibilities:
- *Si hubiera llegado más temprano,* **habría conseguido** *sitio* ("If I had arrived earlier, I would have gotten a seat.")

2. Express unfulfilled desires:
- *Me* **habría encantado** *viajar el año pasado, pero tuve mucho trabajo* ("I would have loved to travel last year, but I had a lot of work.")

3. Talk about imaginary situations:
- *La fiesta* **habría estado** *más divertida con otro tipo de música* ("The party would have been more fun with another type of music.")

4. Express that we agree, or not, with the past actions of other people:
- *María renunció al trabajo, y yo* **habría hecho** *lo mismo* ("María quit her job, and I would have done the same.")

To conjugate verbs in *condicional compuesto,* follow this structure:

yo	habría	
tú	habrías	
él/ella	habría	participio del verbo principal
nosotros/nosotras	habríamos	
vosotros/vosotras	habríais	
ellos/ellas	habrían	

Exercises

1. Go back to the short story at the beginning and reread it. Then, answer the following questions in Spanish.
    a. ¿Qué dice el hombre con bigote?
    b. ¿Por qué Manuel piensa que le vendría bien una calculadora?
    c. ¿En qué puesto está el padre de Manuel?
    d. ¿Cuál es la primera cosa de la que está seguro el padre de Manuel?
2. Complete the following short story with the correct conjugations of the verbs in the *futuro simple*.
    Te .... *(decir)* lo que .... *(hacer)* en mis vacaciones. .... *(ir)* a Europa y a África. Mi primera parada .... *(ser)* Madrid. Luego, ... *(bajar)* hasta Málaga, en la costa. Finalmente, ... *(tomar)* un buque y .... *(viajar)* por el Mediterráneo hasta llegar a Marruecos. ¡Seguramente, ... *(ser)* las mejores vacaciones de mi vida!
3. Match each pronoun with the corresponding conjugation of the auxiliary verb *haber* to form the *futuro compuesto* tense.
    1. yo   a. habremos
    2. tú   b. habrán
    3. él/ella   c. habré
    4. nosotros/nosotras   d. habrá

      5. vosotros/vosotras   e. habrás
      6. ellos/ellas   f. habréis

4. Decide whether each sentence is conjugated in *futuro simple* or in *futuro compuesto*.

    a. Para el año que viene ya **me habré graduado**.

    b. Manuel **visitará** Barcelona.

    c. Daniela y Felipe **estudiarán** toda la tarde.

    d. No sé qué **habrán comido** mis gatos.

5. Decide whether the following statements are true or false. Correct the false ones.

    a. *Condicional simple* is used to politely ask something.

    b. *Condicional simple* is used to talk about an action that is currently taking place.

    c. *Condicional compuesto* is used to talk about imaginary situations.

    d. *Condicional compuesto* is conjugated with the verb *tener*.

Chapter 10: Prepositions and Conjunctions

Short Story: La procesión

José siente un peso inmenso sobre su espalda. A esta altura del recorrido, ya está completamente **agotado**. Pero no puede **darse por vencido**. Toda la cofradía entrenó durante meses para este momento. Sabe que puede hacerlo.

A su izquierda, José ve a Antonio, otro de los portadores. Se conocen desde pequeños, porque vivían a dos casas de distancia en uno de los barrios más humildes de Málaga. Él también parece cansado.

No es para menos. La procesión, que ya está volviendo a la Catedral de la Encarnación, duró ocho horas. Es mucho tiempo para estar cargando una estatua gigante sobre las espaldas. José no está seguro, pero la imagen de Jesús el Rico, con su trono, su cruz y sus velas, debe pesar unos tres mil kilos. No por nada hacen falta doscientos hombres para levantarla. "Es obvio que el **escultor** no era portador", piensa José, mientras acomoda el paso para distribuir mejor su carga.

La lluvia ha sido un tema importante ese día. Un **suelo húmedo** es un suelo **resbaladizo**. Precisamente, eso hace más lenta su marcha, por lo que todos han tenido que resignarse a pasar media hora más con el Cristo **a cuestas**. Sin embargo, José siente que le ha tocado la mejor parte. En su puesto, en el flanco derecho, la lluvia lo ha refrescado durante el recorrido.

De pronto, José nota que ya llegaron a destino. La catedral está justo enfrente: puede ver perfectamente el escenario que han montado. En él, a la derecha de los representantes comunales, hay un hombre vestido íntegramente de negro, con una **capucha** que le cubre el **rostro**. Ese hombre es Pablo, el hermano de José, **preso** desde hace un año por delito de **estafa**. José no se engaña: el Ponzi de Pablo ha tenido muchas víctimas. Él inclusive. Durante mucho tiempo le guardó rencor por eso. Pero sigue siendo su hermano.

José **atestigua** la firma de los decretos. Entonces, prepara la espalda para soportar la puesta en funcionamiento de la **maquinaria**. Jesús el Rico mueve su mano robótica y hace la señal de la cruz. Cuando termine, Pablo será oficialmente un hombre libre. Será otro de los beneficiados por el indulto anual que Jesús el Rico de Málaga ejerce sobre uno de los presos de la ciudad en Semana Santa.

Antonio también conoce a Pablo de toda la vida. Él ha escapado de su estafa, por suerte. José lo mira y nota que está llorando. Justo entonces detecta, en su mirada, un punto nuboso, **fuera de foco**. Sus manos están ocupadas en soportar el peso de la imagen, así que no puede usarlas para limpiarse. Se limita a mirar el suelo. Entonces deja caer una lágrima sobre el suelo húmedo, justo entre sus pies cansados.

Vocabulary List

Spanish	English
agotado, agotada	exhausted
darse por vencido	give up
el escultor, la escultora	sculptor
el suelo	ground

húmedo, húmeda	wet
resbaladizo, resbaladiza	slippery
a cuestas	on somebody's back
la capucha	hood
el rostro	face
el preso, la presa	prisoner
la estafa	scam
atestiguar	witness, attest
la maquinaria	machinery
fuera de foco	out of focus

Grammar Section

We've already seen verbs, adverbs, adjectives, nouns, pronouns, determiners... But we are still missing two types of words that are very necessary to have fluid conversations in Spanish. These are the "linking" words—those that are inserted between all the others. In this chapter, we will look at:

- prepositions;
- conjunctions; and
- idioms with prepositions and conjunctions.

Prepositions

Prepositions, by themselves, have no meaning. They make up a group of words that link other words, such as nouns, verbs, and pronouns. Prepositions have several senses: they can indicate origin, destination, location, direction, duration, starting point, means, reasons... and much more!

The good thing about these words is that they are invariable, i. e., they don't suffer any alteration of person, gender, or number. In Spanish, there are 23 prepositions, although we currently use only 19. Four (*cabe, so, versus,* and *vía*) are archaic.

Unfortunately, for the most part, prepositions don't have a literal translation into English. Therefore, below we will see a list of the 19 most used prepositions in Spanish with some possible equivalents. Later in this chapter, we'll go into each of the most used prepositions and see example sentences.

Preposición	Traducción
a	at, to
ante	before
bajo	under
con	with
contra	against
de	from, of
desde	from, after, since
durante	during, for
en	in, within
entre	between
hacia	towards, to, around

hasta	by, until
mediante	through
para	for
por	by, in, at
según	according to
sin	without
sobre	above, on
tras	behind, after

Spanish most common prepositions

Now, let's see in detail the uses of the most common prepositions. In addition, we'll see them within an example sentence.

1. A

- Direction: *Me voy a la universidad* ("I'm going to college.")
- Distance: *La tienda está a una calle* ("The store is one block away.")
- Location of something or someone with respect to something else: *Cristina está a mi izquierda* ("Cristina is to my left.")
- Time of day: *Ven a las cuatro en punto* ("Come at four o'clock.")
- Objective: *Estoy dispuesto a hacerlo* ("I'm willing to do it.")

Note: When *a* is followed by the article *el*, they come together to form *al*.

2. Con

- Company: *Carmen vino **con** su esposo* ("Carmen came with her husband.")
- Means or instruments: *Sebastián escribe **con** un bolígrafo* ("Sebastián writes with a pen.")

3. De
- Possession: *Este vestido es **de** Paula* ("This dress belongs to Paula.")
- Material or content: *Es una caja **de** bombones* ("It's a box of chocolates.")
- Starting point: *Viajé **de** Santiago a Lima* ("I traveled from Santiago to Lima.")
- Origin or procedence: *Roberto es **de** Argentina* ("Roberto is from Argentina.")

Note: When *de* is followed by the article *el*, they come together to form *del*.

4. En
- Place: *Estoy **en** España* ("I'm in Spain.")
- Time: *Mi cumpleaños es **en** mayo* ("My birthday is in May.")
- Means of transportation: *Viajo **en** tren* ("I travel by train.")

5. Para
- Recipient: *Esto es **para** ti* ("This is for you.")
- Destination: *Voy **para** allá* ("I'm going there.")

6. Por
- Person who did something: *El paciente fue atendido **por** el médico* ("The patient was seen by the doctor.")
- Duration: *Te esperé **por** tres horas* ("I waited for you for three hours.")
- Cause: ***Por** tu talento, ganamos el partido* ("Because of your talent, we won the match.")
- Transit: *Pasaré **por** el supermercado de camino al trabajo* ("I will stop by the grocery store on my way to work.")

7. Sin

- Lack: *El plato del perro está **sin** comida* ("The dog's bowl is without food.")

Conjunctions

Conjunctions are words that connect other words and sentences. These can be *coordinantes* ("coordinating") or *subordinantes* ("subordinating").

Conjunciones coordinantes join elements of the same hierarchy. Let's see them in detail in the table below.

Conjunciones coordinantes		
Type	Use	Examples
Copulativas (copulative)	To indicate addition	*y* (*e* when the next word begins with I or HI) *como* *tanto* *cuanto* *así*
Adversativas (adversative)	To oppose ideas	*pero* *sino*
Disyuntivas (disjunctive)	To indicate alternation	*o* (*u* when the next word begins with O or HO)

Let's see some example sentences with *conjunciones coordinantes*:

- *Tengo dos hijos, Gabriel **y** Simón* ("I have two sons, Gabriel and Simon.")
- *No tengo dos perros, **sino** tres* ("I don't have two dogs, but three.")
- *¿Qué prefieres, la carne **o** el pollo?* ("What do you prefer, beef or chicken?")

Now, it's the turn of *conjunciones subordinantes*. In these cases, one of the elements has a higher hierarchy than the other.

Conjunciones subordinantes		
Type	Use	Examples
Causales (causal)	To express the reason for the main sentence	*porque* *como*
Comparativas (comparative)	To compare the subordinated sentence with the main sentence	*que* *como si*
Concesivas (concessive)	To oppose the main sentence	*aunque* *si bien*
Consecutivas (consecutive)	To express consequence	*que*

Let's see some example sentences:
- *Llegué más tarde **porque** se demoró el autobús* ("I arrived late because the bus was delayed.")
- *Lo dulce me gusta más **que** lo salado* ("I like sweet more than salty.")
- *El té me gusta, **aunque** prefiero el café* ("I like tea, although I prefer coffee.")
- *Estoy tan aburrida **que** no sé qué hacer* ("I'm so bored I don't know what to do.")

Idioms

Now, let's see some idiomatic expressions, or idioms, that have prepositions and conjunctions.

1. Irse por las ramas

Irse por las ramas (literally, "to go through the branches") is an idiom used when someone is avoiding a topic or when someone is not going to the point of what they are saying. The equivalent idiom in English is "to beat around the bush." Let's see an example:

- *Te estás **yendo por las ramas**. Cuéntame exactamente lo que ocurrió* ("You're beating around the bush. Tell me exactly what happened.")

2. Tener que ver con (alguien/algo)

Tener que ver is used as a synonym for *estar relacionado*. The English equivalent for this idiom would be "to have to do with." Let's look at an example:

- *Mi gato **no tiene nada que ver** con ese jarrón roto* ("My cat has nothing to do with that broken vase.")

3. Dar gato por liebre

Dar gato por liebre (literally, "giving a cat by a hare") refers to cheating someone by giving them something of little value, making them believe that's something better. It's similar to the English idiom "giving a pig in a poke." Let's look at an example:

- *Eres muy ingenuo. ¡Siempre te dan gato por liebre!* ("You are so naive. You always get a pig in a poke!")

4. Tirar la casa por la ventana

This funny expression literally means "to throw the house out the window." It is used when someone makes a large expense, higher than usual. It is often used to talk about big parties:

- *Pienso **tirar la casa por la ventana** cuando me gradúe* ("I plan to throw a big party when I graduate.")

5. Levantarse con el pie izquierdo

This idiom literally means "waking up with the left foot," but the English equivalent is "to get out of the wrong side of the bed." For example:

- *Hoy todo me salió mal. Creo que **me levanté con el pie izquierdo*** ("Today everything went wrong. I think I got off on the wrong foot.")

6. Estar como una cabra

Estar como una cabra (literally, "to be like a goat") means to be mad or off your head. For example:

- *Cruzó la calle con el semáforo en rojo. ¡**Está como una cabra!*** ("He crossed the street with a red light. He's completely mad!")

7. No tener ni pies ni cabeza

This is equivalent to "not being able to make heads or tails." If something *no tiene ni pies ni cabeza* (literally, "has neither feet nor head"), it means that it makes no sense.

- *Lo que estás diciendo **no tiene ni pies ni cabeza*** ("What you are saying has neither head nor tail.")

8. Hablar hasta por los codos

Hablar hasta por los codos (literally, "to speak even through the elbows") is similar to "to talk somebody's head off" or "to talk somebody's ear off," i.e., to talk a lot. For example:

- *Mi sobrino solo tiene tres años, pero **habla hasta por los codos*** ("My nephew is only three, but he talks his head off.")

9. Ponerse manos a la obra

Ponerse manos a la obra means to get to work or get to do what you have to do. For example:

- ***Me pondré manos a la obra** y empezaré a estudiar* ("I'll get to work and start studying.")

10. Sin pelos en la lengua

Someone who speaks *sin pelos en la lengua* ("without hairs in their tongue") is someone who doesn't watch their words, somebody outspoken:

- *Mi abuela, que **no tiene pelos en la lengua**, me dijo que le gustaba más mi antiguo corte de pelo* ("My outspoken grandmother told me she liked my old haircut better.")

What did you think of these funny idioms? Were they helpful in studying the prepositions and conjunctions? Let's see how much you've learned!

Exercises

1. Go back to the short story at the beginning and write down all the prepositions you can find in the first three paragraphs.
2. Decide whether the following statements are true or false. Correct the false ones.
    a. Prepositions in Spanish have an exact translation into English.

b. *Sin* is a conjunction.
c. Conjunctions can be coordinating or subordinating.
d. Adversative conjunctions are used to oppose ideas.
e. Complete the following sentences with the correct preposition, contraction (*al* or *del*), or conjunction.
   a. Almería, ... sur de España, está ...... el mar ...... las montañas.
   b. Ernesto viaja todos los días ...... su casa ...... el trabajo ...... autobús.
   c. Ya no quedan entradas para el concierto, ... este sitio web.
   d. Mi comida favorita no es la paella, ... el gazpacho.
   e. Try to use these four idioms in a sentence:
      i. Tirar la casa por la ventana.
      ii. Hablar hasta por los codos.
      iii. Levantarse con el pie izquierdo.
      iv. No tener ni pies ni cabeza.
f. Find all the idioms in the next dialogue:
   A. *Voy a la tienda de música de la otra calle a comprar unas cuerdas para mi guitarra. ¿Quieres acompañarme?*
   B. *¿A la tienda de música de la otra calle? ¡Mejor no! El dependiente es... particular.*
   A. *¿Qué quieres decir? ¿Te ha intentado vender gato por liebre?*
   B. *No, no tiene que ver con eso. Es solo que habla hasta por los codos. La última vez que fui a comprar a su tienda, me contó que era un músico muy famoso hace algunas décadas, y que tiraba la casa por la ventana cada noche. ¿Te imaginas? ¿Un músico muy famoso?*
   A. *Suena como alguien que está como una cabra. ¿Cómo se llama?*
   B. *Claudio "el Magnífico", dice que lo llamaban. Un apodo sin pies ni cabeza, como verás.*

A. ¿Claudio "el Magnífico"? ¿El famosísimo guitarrista retirado?

Chapter 11: Interrogative, Affirmative, and Negative sentences

Short Story: La vaca

El oficial García peina su cabello hacia atrás con la mano. Después **suspira**.

—Vamos **de vuelta** —dice García—. ¿Cómo se llama usted?

—Me llamo Segundo Sánchez —responde el **interrogado** con seguridad.

—Muy bien —dice García—. Eso ya ha quedado **asentado** en el registro. ¿A qué se dedica?

—Soy veterinario —contesta Sánchez.

—¿Cuál es su especialidad? —pregunta García.

—**Ganado** vacuno —contesta Sánchez, sin dudar.

García acerca su silla a la mesa para apoyar los **codos**. Siempre odió que las sillas de la sala de interrogatorios no tuvieran **apoyabrazos**. Son demasiado incómodas.

—¿Qué estaba haciendo anoche en el campo del señor Obrador? —pregunta García.

—Estaba atendiendo una de sus vacas —contesta Sánchez—. Estaba **tumbada** desde hacía horas. Creían que estaba enferma.

—¿Y qué averiguó usted? —pregunta García.

—Que sí, que estaba enferma —contesta Sánchez.

—¿Cuál era su **enfermedad**? —continúa García.

—Un problema estomacal, casi **con seguridad** —responde Sánchez—. Se soluciona con un poco de medicación.

—Hasta aquí, **todo en orden** —dice García—. Pero usted no vino a la estación de policía por esto.

—No —contesta Sánchez—. Yo quiero denunciar un caso de robo de ganado.

—¿Por qué quiere denunciar eso? —pregunta García.

—Porque esa vaca desapareció —responde Sánchez.

—Eso lo entiendo —dice García—. Pero... A ver, ¿cómo desapareció esa vaca?

—Bueno, yo le puedo contar lo que vi —contesta Sánchez—. **Averiguar** qué ocurrió depende de ustedes.

—Agradezco que nos deje esa parte a nosotros —responde García, con **un deje de ironía**—. De acuerdo, cuente.

—Era de noche —dice Sánchez—. Yo estaba atendiendo a la vaca. Estaba solo, porque Obrador había vuelto a su casa a buscar una buena **linterna**. Y entonces empecé a ver luces.

—¿Qué tipo de luces? —pregunta García.

—Luces brillantes. Venían desde el cielo, desde una nube negra —responde Sánchez—. Y había también un sonido extraño. Un **pitido**.

—¿Usted estaba solo? —pregunta García.

—Sí, completamente solo —contesta Sánchez—. Y después... Bueno, una especie de reflector iluminó a la vaca. Y la vaca subió hacia el cielo, hasta la nube negra. Cuando llegó a la nube, desapareció.

—¿Qué dice Obrador de todo esto? —contesta García, mientras masajea su hombro derecho.

—No lo sé —responde Sánchez—. No hablé con él. Vine directo hacia aquí.

—Muchas gracias, Sánchez —dice García—. Ha **cumplido con su deber**. Puede retirarse.

Vocabulary List

Spanish	English
de vuelta	back, again
interrogado, interrogada	questioned
asentado, asentada	settled
el ganado	cattle
el codo	elbow
el apoyabrazos	armrest
tumbado, tumbada	lying down
la enfermedad	illness
con seguridad	safely
todo en orden	all good
averiguar	figure out
un deje de ironía	a hint of irony
la linterna	flashlight
el pitido	beep

| cumplir con el deber | fulfill the duty |

Grammar Section

Questions are everywhere, don't you think? Knowing how to ask questions in Spanish is necessary to have a fluent conversation. Thus, by the end of this next-to-last chapter, you'll master:

- yes/no questions;
- wh- questions;
- rhetorical questions;
- tag questions;
- polite questions; and
- affirmative and negative statements.

Let's get to it!

Yes/no questions

There are many types of questions in Spanish. Yes/no questions are (as you have no doubt noticed) the ones that can be answered with *sí* or *no*. Best of all: there's nothing complex here. In English, the structure of a question is not the same as the structure of a statement, but in Spanish, yes/no questions have the same word order as affirmative sentences. To distinguish one another in writing, you have to add the opening question mark (¿). When talking, you just give it a question intonation towards the end of the sentence. Let's look at some examples:

- *Esta casa es grande* (affirmative statement: "This house is big.")
- *¿Esta casa es grande?* (question: "Is this house big?")
- *María tiene treinta años* (affirmative statement: "María is 30 years old.")
- *¿María tiene treinta años?* (question: "Is María 30 years old?")

Open questions

Now, it's time to talk about open questions. Formulating them can be a bit more complicated than yes/no questions. In this case, adding an interrogative intonation at the end of the sentence is not enough. Open questions have their own structure. Don't worry, though; with practice, you will master them all!

When you ask an open question, you are not expecting the person to answer *sí* or *no*: you are waiting for the person to answer with another phrase, giving you specific information. In English, these questions are called "wh- questions" because they start with interrogative pronouns whose first letters are WH (except "how," of course). In Spanish, the interrogative pronouns are the following (note how they all have an accent mark):

Pronombre interrogativo	Traducción
qué	what
quién	who
cuándo	when
cómo	how
dónde	where
por qué	why

Let's see some example sentences with the interrogative pronouns in Spanish:

- *¿Dónde está Juan?* ("Where is Juan?")
- *¿Quién es ese hombre?* ("Who's that man?")
- *¿Cuándo llegaste?* ("When did you come?")
- *¿Cómo está el clima?* ("How is the weather?")
- *¿Dónde dejé mis llaves?* ("Where did I leave my keys?")
- *¿Por qué no fuiste a trabajar?* ("Why didn't you go to work?")

Tag questions

Tag questions are those small questions attached to a statement's end. They have the particularity that they say the opposite thing in the main sentence; if a sentence is affirmative, the question will be negative, and vice versa. Tag questions transform a statement into a question, and in English, they are used often. For example, in the sentence "He said he'd come tomorrow, didn't he?", "didn't he?" is a tag question.

Let's see the most common tag questions in Spanish, with an example sentence below each one.

1. *¿No?*

- *Tu hijo se llama Fernando, ¿no?* ("Your son's name is Fernando, right?")

2. *¿O no?*

- *Ya conoces Colombia, ¿o no?* ("You've been to Colombia, haven't you?")

3. *¿Verdad?*

- *Este lugar es muy bonito, ¿verdad?* ("This place is very nice, isn't it?")

4. *¿Cierto? / ¿No es cierto?*

- *Mañana es lunes, ¿cierto?* ("Tomorrow's Monday, right?")

Another group of tag questions in Spanish is made up by the ones used after an imperative sentence. For example:

1. *¿Sí?*

- *Pórtate bien, ¿sí?* "(Be good, okay?")

2. *¿De acuerdo?*

- *Limpia tu dormitorio, ¿de acuerdo?* ("Clean your room, okay?")

3. *¿Vale?*

- *Te espero a las siete, ¿vale?* ("I'll wait for you at seven, alright?")

4. *¿Lo harás?*

- *Llámame mañana, ¿lo harás?* ("Call me tomorrow, will you"?)

Rhetorical questions

A rhetorical question is a question in which the speaker is not looking for an answer; instead, they are trying to emphasize what's being said. Usually, the answer is implicit within the question. Many times, they are used in arguments and ironically.

Some examples of rhetorical questions in Spanish are:

- *¿Cuándo terminará esta pesadilla?* ("When will this nightmare end?")
- *¿De dónde sacaste esa idea?* ("Where did you get that idea from?")
- *¿Cuántas veces te lo tengo que decir?* ("How many times do I have to tell you?")
- *¿Por qué siempre tienes razón?* ("Why are you always right?")
- *¿Quién sino tú me iba a ayudar?* ("Who but you was going to help me?")
- *¿Cómo puedes decir eso?* ("How can you say that?")

Polite questions

One of the most common ways to ask a question politely is by adding the verb *disculpar* ("to excuse") at the beginning of the interrogation. Of course, you will conjugate the verb depending on the person you are talking to. Let's see some examples:

- *Disculpe, ¿me puede decir qué hora es?* ("Excuse me, can you tell me what time it is?")
- *Disculpad, chicos, ¿sabéis dónde queda la calle Independencia?* ("Excuse me, guys, do you know where Independencia street is?")

Another expression you can use instead of *disculpar* is *perdonar*.

- *Perdona, ¿tú trabajas aquí?* ("Excuse me, do you work here?")

Now, there are a few basic expressions that you can use when you want to ask polite questions. Some of them are:

1. *¿Te importaría....?* ("Would you mind...?")
    - *¿Te importaría alcanzarme el azúcar?* ("Would you mind passing me the sugar?")

2. *¿Qué te parece si...?* ("What do you think if...?")
   - *¿Qué te parece si vamos a un restaurante el sábado?* ("How about if we go to a restaurant on Saturday?")
3. *¿Te gustaría...?* ("Would you like...?")
   - *¿Te gustaría acompañarme a hacer la compra?* ("Would you like to go shopping with me?")
4. *¿Podrías...?* ("Could you...")
   - *¿Podrías darme un kilo de bananas, por favor?* ("Could you give me a kilo of bananas, please?")

Negative statements

To make a negative sentence, you have to take into account a series of negation adverbs. Adverbs of negation modify verbs, adjectives or other adverbs. They are invariable, i.e, they are always written in the same way. There are four negation adverbs in Spanish:

Negation Adverb	Translation
no	no
nunca	never
jamás	never
tampoco	either

Let's see some example sentences with these negation adverbs:
- **No** *quiero comer pizza esta noche* ("I don't want to eat pizza tonight.")
- **Nunca** *me fui de vacaciones a las montañas* ("I never went on holidays to the mountains.")
- **Jamás** *he tenido un perro como mascota* ("I've never had a dog as a pet.")
- *A mí* **tampoco** *me parece que sea una buena idea* ("I don't think it's a good idea either.")

However, negation adverbs are not the only words we can use to form negative sentences in Spanish. There are also some useful pronouns, like *nadie* ("nobody") and *nada* ("nothing"), adjectives like *ningún* or *ninguna* ("none"), conjunctions like *ni* ("nor"), and expressions like *ni siquiera* ("not even"). Normally, these words go together with the adverbs of negation that we just saw, forming double negations.

Let's see some example sentences:

- *No fue **ninguno** de los chicos a la fiesta* ("None of the guys went to the party.") You could also say ***Ninguno*** *de los chicos fue a la fiesta.*
- *Este vecindario es aburrido, ¡**nunca** pasa **nada**!* ("This neighborhood is boring, nothing ever happens!")
- *Esta chaqueta **no** es de **nadie** que yo conozca* ("This jacket doesn't belong to anyone that I know.")
- ***No, ni siquiera*** *se despidió* ("No, he didn't even say goodbye.")
- ***No*** *me gusta este vestido **ni** tampoco aquel* ("I don't like this dress and I don't like that one either.")

Affirmative statements

Just as there are negative sentences, there are affirmative ones. The most important words to keep in mind are the following:

Affirmative Words	Translation
sí	yes
siempre	always
también	also
algo	something
alguien	somebody

algún, alguno, alguna	some
por supuesto	of course
claro	sure
obvio	obvious
desde luego	for sure

Let's see some example sentences with these words:

- **Por supuesto** *que me gusta el rock. ¡**Siempre** estoy escuchando **algún** disco!* (Of course I like rock. I'm always listening to some record!")

- *Juan es **alguien** que ama la fotografía: **siempre** va a la playa y toma **algunas** imágenes* ("Juan is someone who loves photography: he always goes to the beach and takes some pictures.")

- **Desde luego**, *a Luisa **también** le gustaría adoptar un perro algún día* ("Of course, Luisa would also like to adopt a dog some day.")

Exercises

1. Go back to the short story at the beginning and answer the following questions in Spanish:

    a. ¿Qué hacía el señor Sánchez en el campo del señor Obrador?

    b. ¿Cuál es la profesión del señor Sánchez?

    c. ¿Qué problema afectaba a la vaca y cómo se resolvió?

    d. ¿Por qué el señor Obrador no estaba con el señor Sánchez?

2. Below are four answers to four open (or wh-) questions. Following the examples, write down the corresponding question:

    a. Lucía se siente un poco cansada. ¿*Cómo se siente Lucía?*
    b. Es mi esposo.
    c. Los chicos están en el colegio.
    d. La última vez que vi a Tomás fue ayer.
3. Decide whether the following statements are true or false. Correct the false ones.
    a. Interrogative pronouns in Spanish are used to make yes/no questions.
    b. Rhetorical questions are those to which we don't expect an answer.
    c. *Sí, siempre* and *por supuesto* are used to make affirmative statements in Spanish.
    d. Adverbs of negation are written differently depending on the gender of the word they modify.
4. Complete the following dialogue to form a polite conversation between two people. Use the following words: *gustaría, disculpe, por favor, podría.*
    A. ...., ¿usted trabaja en esta tienda?
    B. Sí. Dígame en qué puedo ayudarla.
    A. ¿......... indicarme dónde están los probadores, ... ?
    B. Claro. Están al fondo de la tienda. ¿*le .... que la acompañe?*
5. In the following text, select the correct negation word in each case.
    Florencia mira el reloj. (Nunca/No) es tan temprano como pensaba. Si (no/nunca) se apresura, llegará tarde al trabajo. Se sube a su coche y, como hay mucho tráfico, decide tomar una ruta alternativa. (Ni siquiera/Jamás) ha ido por esa zona. No parece haber (ninguno/nada) por allí: es una calle desierta. (Nada/No) hay ningún coche y (tampoco/nunca) hay (nadie/ningún) caminando. ¡(Ni siquiera/Nunca) tiene que esperar, porque (ni/no) hay (ningún/ninguno) semáforo! Llega a su trabajo más temprano que de costumbre. Ahora, ya sabe qué ruta debe tomar cada día.

Chapter 12: Reporting Information (Indirect Speech)

Short Story: La conversación

El oficial García se acerca a la **máquina de café**. Aprieta un botón y coloca un **vaso desechable** debajo del pico vertedor. Después espera.

—¿Qué te dijo Sánchez? —pregunta el sargento Moreno.

—No me vas a creer —responde García, mientras retira el vaso de la máquina. Después bebe un sorbo de café negro. Es el segundo del día.

—**Anda**, dime —dice Moreno—. **No me obligues a leer** el reporte.

—Sánchez dijo que vio una **abducción extraterrestre** —responde García, mientras se encoge de hombros.

—Hombre, no digas tonterías —contesta Moreno.

—Es en serio —dice García—. Dijo que una luz se llevó a la vaca que estaba atendiendo. La vaca enferma de Obrador.

—¿Y Obrador qué opina? —pregunta Moreno.

—No sé, todavía no he hablado con él —contesta García—. Lo fueron a buscar. Dicen que **está en camino**.

Moreno se quita la **gorra** y se limpia el **sudor** de la **frente**. El aire acondicionado de la estación está roto, y el lugar no tiene buena circulación de aire. No es una buena época para hacer **trabajo de escritorio**.

—No lo puedo creer —dice Moreno—. Sánchez parecía un hombre **serio**. Veterinario. ¿Tú qué hiciste?

—Hice lo que pude —responde García—. Le pregunté si estaba solo. Le pregunté cómo eran las luces.

—¿Y él qué hizo? —pregunta Moreno.

—Me dijo que esstaba solo, que las luces eran brillantes... —contesta García—. Todo ese **rollo**. No sé, tampoco quería hacerlo sentir mal. Por lo menos, no antes de hablar con Obrador. Quiero tener una **denuncia** concreta antes de interrogarlo.

Moreno apoya la **cadera** contra la pared para descansar los pies. Después coloca ambos **pulgares** en sus bolsillos y suspira.

—¿Qué crees que dirá Obrador? —pregunta Moreno, mirando al frente.

—Me dirá que le falta una vaca —responde García.

Vocabulary List

Spanish	English
la máquina de café	coffee machine
el vaso desechable	disposable cup
anda	come on
(no) obligar a alguien a hacer algo	(not) make someone do something
la abducción extraterrestre	alien abduction
estar en camino	be on the way
la gorra	cap

el sudor	sweat
la frente	forehead
el trabajo de escritorio	desk job
serio, seria	reliable
el rollo	yarn
la denuncia	complaint
la cadera	hip
el pulgar	thumb

Grammar Section

Direct and indirect speech are two ways to quote or reproduce a message from someone else – or even yourself! They exist both in English and Spanish, but each language has its own characteristics. Direct speech is the style in which the speaker reproduces word by word what someone else said without modifying it. It is marked graphically with dashes of dialogue (–) or with quotation marks (" "). Indirect speech is the style in which the speaker relates what was said – but in their own words. It requires the interpretation of the message, which is altered in its form, but without changing the meaning.

In this chapter, you will:
- understand what direct speech is and when it is used;
- understand what indirect speech is and when it is used;
- learn the differences between direct and indirect speech;
- learn to transform direct speech into indirect speech; and
- learn what happens with questions in indirect speech.

Let's get to it!

What is direct speech?

Direct speech is the reproduction of a message in the same way in which it was said, without alterations or interpretations. In other words, it's quoting a sentence of one's own or someone else's, just the way it was said. In Spanish, there are two graphical ways to indicate what is being said in direct speech: quotation marks and em-dashes (or r*ayas de diálogo*).

Quotation marks

In written text, direct speech can be recognized by quotation marks, which indicate that the words that follow are from another person or have been copied as they were originally written. For example:

- *Ella me dijo: "prefiero cenar fuera"* ("She said, 'I prefer to eat out.'")
- *La ministra declaró: "Me siento satisfecha con mi gestión"* ("The minister declared, 'I am satisfied with my management.'")

Direct speech is widely used in media, especially in journalism, where the use of quotation marks to indicate that someone's words are being used is common. It's also used in academic texts (dissertations, specialized books, research papers, etc.) to point out ideas of other authors. English also uses quotation marks to indicate direct speech. Still, if you pay attention to the examples above, you will see that, in contrast, Spanish uses a colon (:) before the opening quotation mark, while English uses a comma (,).

Em-dashes

Another way to recognize direct speech is by using dashes, which mark the beginning of a dialogue. The dashes indicate that what follows is an exchange between two or more people, which is reproduced verbatim.

For example:

- —*¿Sabes a qué hora llega la jefa hoy?* ("Do you know at what time the boss is arriving today?")
- —*No lo sé* ("I don't know.")
- —*Tal vez no venga...* ("Maybe she's not coming...")
- —*Sí, ayer se sentía mal, así que es probable que hoy se*

quede en casa ("Yea, she was feeling bad yesterday, so she's probably staying home today.")

Dashes are common in written interviews and literary texts such as plays, short stories (like the ones you've read throughout this book!) or novels, which indicate each character's words. This dash doesn't have an extended use in English, where dialogue is also distinguished with quotation marks.

What is indirect speech?

Indirect speech is how we paraphrase a message. That is, the speaker takes a message from someone else (or a previous message by themselves), interprets it, and incorporates it into their speech in their own words.

We must make some changes to transform direct speech into indirect speech. We adapt the original message to the way we want to convey it. Let's see the changes in an example:

- *Hoy no puedo. Pero si tú quieres, mañana paso a verte* ("Today I can't. But if you want, tomorrow I can go visit you.")

In an indirect form, it would change to:

- *Victoria dijo que ese día no podía, pero que al día siguiente pasaría a verme si yo quería* ("Victoria said that she couldn't that day, but that she would come visit me the next day if I wanted.")

Take a look at the following chart to see the changes that we made to transform direct speech into indirect speech:

Direct Speech	Indirect Speech
	me dijo que
hoy	ese día
puedo	podía
tú	yo

quieres	quería
mañana	al día siguiente
paso	pasaría
verte	verme

As we can see, first of all, in indirect speech we add the verb *decir* ("say") and the conjunction *que* ("that"). Other verbs we use to report speech are *anunciar* ("announce"), *explicar* ("explain"), *narrar* ("narrate"), *declarar* ("claim"), *preguntar* ("ask"), *exponer* ("present"), *asentir* ("affirm"), *informar* ("inform"), *citar* ("quote"), and *señalar* ("point").

We can also see that the first person of the direct speech becomes a third person in the indirect speech because the speaker has changed; Victoria is no longer speaking. This is reflected in the conjugation of the verbs and in the pronouns used. Also, the second person of the direct speech (the addressee) becomes the first person because they are the ones doing the talking in the second sentence.

Then, we notice that place and time adverbs are modified to match the new communication situation. The two sentences weren't uttered on the same day, so *hoy* and *mañana* don't mean the same in both contexts – and need to be changed accordingly.

Finally, verbal tenses are also updated to the new communication situation, and apart from person, the *tense* also changes. Now, we'll look at some tense changes in more detail.

How to modify verb tenses in indirect speech

1. Direct speech in *presente*, *futuro* or *pretérito perfecto*: sometime, the tense in indirect speech will not be affected.

- *Me gusta el queso* ("I like cheese," direct speech in the present)
- *Luis dice que le gusta el queso* ("Luis says he likes cheese," indirect speech in the present)

Other times, the tense of the direct speech will change from *presente* to *pretérito imperfecto* in the indirect speech.

- *Llego tarde* ("I'm late," direct speech in the present)
- *Luz dijo que llegaba tarde* ("Luz said she was late," indirect speech in *pretérito imperfecto*)

2. Direct speech in *pretérito indefinido*, *pretérito perfecto* or *pretérito pluscuamperfecto*: indirect speech in *pretérito pluscuamperfecto*.

- *¿Has visitado a tu abuela el domingo pasado* ("Have you visited your grandma last Sunday?" direct speech in *pretérito perfecto*)
- *Tomás me preguntó si había visitado a mi abuela el domingo pasado* ("Tomás asked me if I had visited my grandma last Sunday," indirect speech in *pretérito pluscuamperfecto*)

3. Direct speech in *pretérito imperfecto*: indirect speech in *pretérito imperfecto*.

- *La comida estaba rica* ("The food was good," direct speech in *pretérito imperfecto*)
- *Juan señaló que la comida estaba rica* ("Juan pointed that the food was good," indirect speech in *pretérito imperfecto*)

4. Direct speech in *futuro simple* or *condicional simple*: indirect speech in *condicional simple*.

- *Lo haré la semana que viene* ("I'll do it next week," direct speech in *futuro simple*)
- *Pablo prometió que lo haría la semana que viene* ("Pablo promised he'd do it next week," indirect speech in *condicional simple*)

5. Direct speech in *futuro compuesto* or *condicional compuesto*, indirect speech in *condicional compuesto*.

- *Mañana a esta hora, habremos terminado la tarea* ("By this time tomorrow, we'll have finished the homework," direct speech in *futuro compuesto*)
- *Clara afirmó que para esa hora del día siguiente, habrían terminado la tarea* ("Clara declared that, by that time tomorrow, they would have finished the homework," indirect speech in *condicional compuesto*)

6. Direct speech in *imperativo, presente del subjuntivo* or *condicional compuesto*: indirect speech in *pretérito imperfecto del subjuntivo*.

- *Vayamos al cine* ("Let's go to the cinema," direct speech in *presente del subjuntivo*)
- *María me dijo que fuéramos al cine* ("María said that we should go to the cinema," indirect speech in *pretérito imperfecto del subjuntivo*)

7. Direct speech in *pretérito perfecto del subjuntivo*: indirect speech in *pretérito pluscuamperfecto del subjuntivo*.

- *Quizás Lucas no haya oído el mensaje* ("Maybe Lucas didn't hear the message," direct speech in *pretérito perfecto del subjuntivo*)
- *Javiera supuso que quizás Lucas no hubiese oído el mensaje* ("Javiera guessed that maybe Lucas hadn't heard the message," indirect speech in *pretérito pluscuamperfecto del subjuntivo*)

Questions in indirect speech

To finish the chapter (and this book!), we'll look at what happens with questions in indirect speech. Let's start with an example.

- *¿Cómo estás?* ("How are you doing?")
- *Me preguntó cómo estaba* ("She asked me how I was doing.")

First, as you can see in indirect speech, interrogations lose the question marks. As with other sentences in reported speech, they are introduced by a saying verb, but instead of *que*, they are followed by an interrogation pronoun or adverb, or the conjunction *si*. Let's see some more examples:

- *¿Estás bien?* ("Are you okay?")
- *Le pregunté si estaba bien* ("I asked him if he was okay.")
- *¿Qué te pasó ayer?* ("What happened to you yesterday?")
- *Me preguntó qué me había pasado el día anterior* ("She asked me what had happened to me the day before.")

Note that the *qué* we use when we are reporting questions has an accent, and it's not the same conjunction *que* we use to report statements.

Exercises

1. Go back to the short story at the beginning and answer the following questions in Spanish using reported or indirect speech. Follow the example:

    a. ¿Qué es lo primero que le preguntó el sargento Moreno al oficial García? *Moreno le preguntó qué le había dicho Sánchez.*

    b. ¿Qué le respondió García?

    c. ¿Qué le dijo Moreno a García después de que este le hablara de la abducción extraterrestre?

    d. ¿Qué le preguntó Moreno a García sobre Obrador?

2. Decide whether the following statements are true or false. Correct the false ones.

    a. Direct and indirect speech are used only to reproduce someone else's message.

    b. Direct speech quotes the message said word by word.

    c. Em-dashes and quotation marks are used in English and Spanish to indicate indirect speech.

    d. To change a sentence from direct to indirect speech, first, we need to add a speaking verb plus the conjunction *que*.

3. Go back to the short story in the previous chapter and reread the first few lines. Below, we've transformed those lines of dialogue into reported speech. Complete the blanks with the verbs in the correct conjugation.

    a. García le preguntó a Sánchez cómo ………

    b. Con seguridad, el interrogado …… que se llamaba Segundo Sánchez.

    c. García dijo que eso ya …… en el registro.

    d. Luego, le preguntó a qué ……..

    e. Sánchez contestó que …… veterinario.

    f. García le …… cuál era su especialidad.

4. The following sentences are all in indirect speech. Choose the correct adverb or conjunction so that they make sense:
   a. Le dije a mi padre ...... (que/cuando) me viniera a visitar.
   b. Camila le preguntó a su novia ...... (que/qué) quería comer.
   c. Nos prometieron ...... (si/que) estaría terminado para la semana que viene.
   d. Me preguntó ...... (si/cual) iría al cine al día siguiente.
5. Imagine you had a conversation with a friend. Write it down as if you were telling it to another friend. You can start the following way:

   El lunes pasado le pregunté a María si... Ella me respondió que...

Now that you've finished the last chapter, you can go back and check all the things you've learned from the list at the beginning!

Final Quiz

Congratulations! You've reached the end of the book. We're sure that, by now, you will have learned a lot of Spanish. Now, all that remains is to put it into practice!

But before letting you go, it's time to do a final quiz. In this quiz, we are going to review the last six chapters, where we have seen the *pasado*, *presente* and *futuro* tenses of the Spanish verbs, prepositions and conjunctions, how to ask questions, direct and indirect speech, – and more.

Like in the Mid-Book Quiz, each correct answer is worth 2 points.

- If your final result is between 15 and 20 points: Congratulations! You've mastered the grammar, and the vocabulary needed to be an intermediate Spanish student.
- If your final result is between 10 and 15 points: You're doing very well. However, we recommend you to go back to the chapters that explain the topics you've failed and review them.
- If your final result is less than 10 points: Don't worry; there's no rush. Take your time and reread this book. Once you have done it, repeat this quiz. Be patient and practice a lot. You'll do better soon!

Now, let's get started!

1. What is *presente del indicativo* used for? Three of the following answers are true, and one is false; find the false one.
   a. To talk about situations that will happen in the near future.
   b. To talk about something that is happening right now.
   c. To express a hypothesis.
   d. To talk about things that are always true.

2. Complete with *presente progresivo*.
   a. Tú - caminar
   b. Ella - dormir
   c. Nosotros - salir
   d. Vosotros - dibujar

3. Complete the following dialogue with the past tenses in Spanish.
   A. ¿Qué .... (**hacer** - *pretérito perfecto simple*) el fin de semana?
   B. Nada, no .... (**tener** - *pretérito imperfecto*) muchas ganas de salir. ¿Y tú?
   A. Yo .... (**ir** - *pretérito perfecto simple*) a dar un paseo por la costa. La noche .... (**ser** - *pretérito imperfecto*) perfecta, aunque .... (**hacer** - *pretérito imperfecto*) un poco de frío. .... (**llover** - *pretérito pluscuamperfecto*) un rato antes.
   B. Pero ¿............ (**llevar** - *pretérito pluscuamperfecto*) abrigo?
   A. No. ¡Quizá por eso no .... (**dejar** - *pretérito perfecto*) de estornudar desde entonces!

4. Complete the following short story with the *futuro simple* form of the verbs in brackets. *Juan Pablo .... (hacer) una fiesta este fin de semana. Sus amigos lo .... (ayudar) a planearla y .... (llevar) comida. Juan Pablo .... (encargarse) de la bebida. Todos los conocidos de Juan Pablo están invitados, pero él cree que muchos .... (ir).*

5. Decide if the following sentences are in *condicional simple* or *condicional compuesto*.
   a. Disculpe, ¿me diría la hora?
   b. Habría pagado lo que fuera por ver ese concierto.
   c. Me habría encantado estudiar piano cuando era joven.
   d. Me encantaría viajar al Caribe el próximo año.
6. Choose the correct preposition in each of the following sentences.
   a. Quiero una porción de pizza ..... (que/con) mucho queso.
   b. Martín es el hijo ..... (de/por) Pablo y Susana.
   c. Dormí ..... (mediante/durante) todo el viaje.
   d. Me levanté temprano ..... (por/para) ver el amanecer.
7. Underline the conjunctions in the following sentences, and decide whether they are *conjunciones coordinantes* (coordinating conjunctions) or *conjunciones subordinantes* (subordinating conjunctions).
   a. Cenaré pizza porque me encanta.
   b. Matías y Pedro son mis hermanos.
   c. Voy a estudiar, aunque estoy un poco cansado.
   d. Mi hija menor quiere estudiar Medicina u Odontología.
8. Here you have some typical idioms in Spanish. Match them with their explanation or equivalent idiom in English.

irse por las ramas	to talk somebody's head off
hablar hasta por los codos	to be completely mad
dar gato por liebre	to give a pig in a poke
estar como una cabra	to beat around the bush

9. Complete with the correct interrogative pronoun.
    a. ¿............ se llama tu perro?
    b. ¿............ está tu hermano?
    c. ¿............ es ese hombre?
    d. ¿............ haces esta noche?
10. Decide whether the following statements are true or false. Correct the false ones.
    a. Direct speech consists of interpreting and rewriting someone else's message.
    b. Direct speech is mostly used in the press.
    c. Direct speech can be written with quotes or em-dashes.
    d. Indirect speech is the reproduction of a message in the same way in which it was said, without alterations or interpretations.

Answer Key

Chapter 1

1.
   a. Woman: Mujer: eme-u-jota-e-erre.
   b. Man: Hombre: hace-o-eme-be-erre-e.
   c. Girl: Niña: ene-i-eñe-a.
   d. Dog: Perro: pe-e-doble erre-o.
   e. House: Casa: ce-a-ese-a.

2.
   a. *Cancion*: It should have a tilde in the O because it's an *aguda* word that ends in N: *canción*.
   b. *Papel*: It doesn't need a tilde because it's an *aguda* word that ends in L.
   c. *Tragico*: It should have a tilde in the A because it's an *esdrújula* word: *trágico*.
   d. *Esposa*: It doesn't need a tilde because it's a *grave* word that ends in a vowel.
   e. *Lapiz*: It should have a tilde in the A because it's a *grave* word that ends in Z: *lápiz*.

3. *Tildes* tell us which letter of a word we have to stress when we say it aloud.
4.
    b. They are all graves
5. *Fuerza* is pronounced with a soft R; *rápido* is pronounced with a rolled R; *perro* is also pronounced with a rolled R.
6. We use a softer R for single Rs in the middle of a word; we use the rolled R for Rs at the beginning of words and for double Rs.
7.
    a. *Agua*, because it's the only one in which the U is not silent.
8. All of these sentences are grammatically correct. However, there's one in each pair that is more commonly used. Can you point out which one?
    b. María escribió el libro.
    c. Los alumnos se portan mal.
    e. José preparó la cena.
9.
    a. Mi hermana **juega** muy bien al fútbol.
    b. Tu casa nueva es muy **linda.**
    c. Los niños **tienen** hambre.
    d. Correct.
    e. Siempre desayuno algo **dulce.**
    f. Correct.
    g. Hice las compras, pero me **las** olvidé en el mercado.
    h. Estoy llevando al perro al parque. **Lo** llevo todas las mañanas.
10. True.
11. False. In Spanish, the subject can be left out when it has already been mentioned and it's understood from context.
12. False. In Spanish, the order of a statement doesn't change to turn it into a question. You just need to add the opening and closing marks.

13. True.

14.
- a. El cielo es celeste/azul.
- b. Las bananas son amarillas.
- c. Las hojas de los árboles son verdes.
- d. La sangre es roja.
- e. Las nubes son grises.
- f. Si mezclas blanco y negro, obtienes gris.
- g. Por fuera, el kiwi es marrón.
- h. Las naranjas son naranjas/anaranjadas.

15.
- a. Cuatro.
- b. Ocho.
- c. Catorce.
- d. Trece.
- e. Diecinueve.
- f. Cincuenta.
- g. Sesenta.
- h. Noventa y cinco.

16.
- a. El esposo de mi abuela es mi abuelo.
- b. El hijo de mi tía es mi primo.
- c. La hija de mi madre y mi padre es mi hermana.
- d. El hermano de mi padre es mi tío.
- e. Mi mamá y mi papá son mis padres.
- f. La pareja de mi padre es mi madrastra.

17.
- a. Árbol, porque no es una parte de la casa.
- b. Banana, porque no es un objeto de la casa.
- c. Cerdo, porque no es una fruta.
- d. Pasto, porque no es comida.
- e. Habitación, porque no es un plato.

- f. Blanco, porque no es un método de cocción.
- g. Estrella, porque no es un edificio de una ciudad.
- h. Acera, calle, semáforo, río.
- i. Marzo, porque no es un día de la semana.
- j. Viernes, porque no es el nombre de un mes.

18.
- a. ¿Cómo te llamas?: el nombre.
- b. ¿Cuántos años tienes?: la edad.
- c. ¿A qué te dedicas?: la profesión.
- d. ¿Tienes correo electrónico?: el correo electrónico.
- e. ¿Cuál es tu número de teléfono?: el número de teléfono.
- f. ¿Cuál es tu nombre?: el nombre.
- g. ¿En qué trabajas?: la profesión.
- h. ¿De dónde eres?: la nacionalidad/el lugar de origen.
- i. ¿Tienes móvil?: el número de teléfono

19. _____

20.
- a. El verbo **ser** se utiliza para hablar de estados que duran mucho tiempo o son permanentes.
- b. El verbo **estar** se utiliza para hablar de estados temporales.

21.
- a. Mi nombre **es** Alejandra.
- b. **Soy** de Argentina.
- c. En este momento, **estoy** en Venezuela.
- d. Mi amiga **es** de aquí.
- e. Su nombre **es** María.
- f. **Estamos** de vacaciones juntas.

22.

	AMAR	TEMER	PARTIR
yo	amo	temo	parto
tú	amas	temes	partes
él / ella	ama	teme	parte
nosotros / nosotras	amamos	tememos	partimos
vosotros / vosotras	amáis	teméis	partís
ellos / ellas / ustedes	aman	temen	parten

23.
- a. Alejandro Amenábar nace en 1972.
- b. Cuando su familia se muda a España, tiene un año de edad.
- c. En la universidad estudió Imagen y Sonido. No, no terminó la carrera.
- d. La película que tiene como protagonista a Nicole Kidman es de terror y suspense.
- e. En los últimos años ha hecho películas, video clips de música y series de televisión.

Chapter 2

1.
- a. Cien más treinta y cinco es ciento treinta y cinco.
- b. Quinientos sesenta menos veinte es quinientos cuarenta.

- c. Diez mil cien más cuatro mil setecientos es catorce mil ochocientos.
- d. Doscientos veinticinco por cinco es mil trescientos cincuenta.
- e. Un millón dividido dos coma cinco es cuatrocientos mil.

2.
- a. En el año mil novecientos setenta y cinco, se vendieron quinientos cincuenta y seis camisetas, doscientos dos sombreros y cincuenta y nueve bolsos.
- b. En el año mil novecientos ochenta y seis, se vendieron doscientos ochenta y nueve camisetas, doscientos diez sombreros y trescientos cincuenta y nueves bolsos.
- c. En el año mil novecientos noventa y tres, se vendieron cincuenta y seis camisetas, ciento noventa y cinco sombreros y quinientos noventa y ocho bolsos.
- d. En el año dos mil siete, se vendieron setenta camisetas, doscientos siete sombreros y ochocientos ochenta y dos bolsos.

3.
- a. En el año 1975 se vendieron más bolsos que sombreros. Falso: En el año 1975 se vendieron más sombreros que bolsos.
- b. Se vendieron más bolsos en 2007 que en 1993. Verdadero.
- c. En 1986 y 2007 se vendió casi la misma cantidad de sombreros. Verdadero.
- d. El año en el que más bolsos se vendieron fue 1993. Falso: El año en el que más bolsos se vendieron fue 2007.

4.
- a. Son las nueve y veinticinco.
- b. Cinco minutos.

c. Es a las nueve y media.
5. "De lunes a viernes, me levanto a las...".

Chapter 3

1.
   a. Silvia y Alberto pasean por un barrio comercial de la ciudad.
   b. La historia transcurre durante la noche.
   c. En la historia se mencionan conejos, perros, palomas, ratas y ratones.
   d. La aventura no dura mucho porque una niña recoge a la coneja.

2.
   a. False. Grammatical gender is a property of languages used to divide nominal elements into classes.
   b. True.
   c. False. In Spanish, there are two grammatical genders: masculine and feminine.
   d. True.

3. Complete the sentences with these endings: -TUD; -OR; -SIÓN; -A; -MA; -O. Provide an example of each.
   a. Most nouns ending in -A are feminine, for example *manta*.
   b. Most nouns ending in -O are masculine, for example *lago*.
   c. Other typically feminine endings are -TUD (for example: *gratitud*), and -SIÓN (for example: *pasión*).
   d. Other typically masculine endings are -OR (for example: *dolor*), and -MA (for example: *problema*)

4. *favorito; la; el; muchos; cómoda; la; la; una; clara; pintadas; oscuro; cómoda; ella; preferida; la; un; él; doblada.*

5. _____

Chapter 4

1. ella, lo, todas, eso, tú, les, los, quiénes, todos, ese, el que, esos, se, cualquiera, le.
2.
    a. False. Pronouns are the words we use to replace names or nouns in a sentence.
    b. True.
    c. False. Pronouns also serve to refer to elements that function as antecedents of a topic.
3.
    a. Nosotras.
    b. Lo.
    c. Vosotras/ustedes.
    d. Mí.
4. Choose the correct possessive pronoun:
    a. Suyas.
    b. Nuestro.
    c. Los suyos.
    d. Mía/tuya
5. Write one sentence using each of the following pronouns:
    a. Saludó a cuanta gente se cruzó.
    b. Le ofrecí varios sabores, pero no le gusta ninguno.
    c. No hace falta que traigas azúcar para el pastel. Hay bastante.
    d. De todos los alumnos que dieron el examen, un tercio desaprobó.

Chapter 5

1.
    c. Poco. It's replacing an adverb.
    d. Alto. It's replacing a noun.
    e. Bajo. It's replacing an adverb.

f. Azul. It's replacing a noun

2.
   a. True.
   b. False. In Spanish, the adjective is generally placed after the noun it's modifying.
   c. False. Demonstrative and possessive adjectives come before the noun.
   d. True.

3.
   a. Before.
   b. After.
   c. After.
   d. Before.

4.
   a. Superiority: "más + adjetivo/adverbio + que": Corro más rápido que mis rivales.
   b. Inferiority: "menos + adjetivo/adverbio + que": Es menos peleador que su hermano
   c. Equality: "tan + adjetivo/adverbio + como" or "igual de adjetivo/adverbio que": Mis hijas son igual de inteligentes.
   d. Positive superlative: "el/la/los/las + más + adjetivo": Buenos Aires es la más divertida de todas las ciudades que conozco.
   e. Negative superlative: "el/la/los/las + menos + adjetivo": Aunque el transporte público es el menos organizado.

5.
   a. 2
   b. 4
   c. 1
   d. 3

Chapter 6

1. <u>El</u> viaje; <u>La</u> maleta; <u>Una</u> vida; <u>una</u> maleta; <u>una</u> vida; <u>las</u> playeras; <u>una</u> bola; <u>los</u> calcetines; <u>los</u> pantalones; <u>Un</u> abrigo; <u>una</u> chaqueta; <u>un</u> sobretodo; <u>un</u> saco; <u>la</u> chaqueta; <u>las</u> demás prendas; <u>la</u> habitación; <u>la</u> persona; <u>la</u> relación; <u>lo</u> necesario; <u>unos</u> zapatos; <u>la</u> ropa; <u>la</u> maleta; <u>la</u> ropa; <u>la</u> maleta; <u>la</u> cama; <u>las</u> playeras; <u>los</u> suéteres; <u>los</u> pantalones; <u>el</u> espacio; <u>las</u> prendas; <u>los</u> calcetines, <u>la</u> ropa interior; <u>la</u> chaqueta; <u>la</u> maleta; <u>los</u> zapatos; <u>el</u> trabajo; <u>una</u> ciudad; <u>los</u> cajones; <u>la</u> habitación; <u>una</u> bufanda; <u>el</u> cuello.

2.
    a. True.
    b. False. *Lo* is a neuter article, it carries no gender.
    c. True.
    d. False. Definite articles are used to talk about things that are known to the people involved in the conversation.

3.
    a. Lo bello de la vida es compartirla con los seres queridos.
    b. María se desesperó ante lo difícil del problema.
    c. Debieron cancelar la excursión por lo frío del día.
    d. Lo simple de la vida en el campo resulta muy atractivo.

4. una; un; el; una; un; la; los; la; el; el; los; la; el; el; los; el; el; los; un.

Mid-Book Quiz

1.
    a. Mil setecientos treinta y cinco.
    b. Diecinueve mil quinientos ochenta y tres.
    c. Mil setecientas treinta y cinco vacas.
    d. Diecinueve mil quinientas ochenta y tres vacas.

2. ¿Qué hora es?; ¿Tienes hora?; ¿Puedes decirme la hora?
   a. Son las doce menos cuarto de la mañana.
   b. Son las cuatro y diez de la tarde.
3. Are the following nouns masculine or feminine? Decide by choosing the correct article
   a. la solución
   b. el problema
   c. la foto
   d. la tortuga
   e. la lumbre
   f. la mano
   g. el pie
4. It means that all nouns have gender, and that the pronouns, articles and adjectives around them have to reflect that gender. It is the need to change a word to make it match a grammatical feature of another word, to which it's syntactically connected.
5. What is the bolded pronoun replacing in each case?
   a. María.
   b. Tu hermano, un rompecabezas.
   c. Estás enojado.
   d. Mi madre.
6. Complete with the corresponding demonstrative pronoun.
   a. aquella.
   b. ese.
   c. aquel.
   d. Estas.
7. After the noun. Demonstrative and possessive adjectives; limiting adjectives; adjectives that describe an essential quality of the noun; and adjectives that have a change in meaning are placed before the noun.
8.
   Superiority: "más + adjetivo/adverbio + que"
   Inferiority: "menos + adjetivo/adverbio + que"

Equality: "tan + adjetivo/adverbio + como"
Positive superlative: "el/la/los/las + más + adjetivo"

9.
- a. indefinido.
- b. definido.
- c. definido.
- d. definido/indefinido.

10. Match the common saying in the left with their meanings in the right:
- a. 4
- b. 3
- c. 1
- d. 2

Chapter 7

1. es; piensan; está; sitúan; hay; lleva
2. tenemos; estamos; decimos; hacemos; somos
3. está yendo; estás teniendo; están construyendo; está haciendo
4. siendo; comiendo; haciendo; bailando
5.
   - a. True.
   - b. False. The present indicative can be used to talk about situations that are going to happen in the near future.
   - c. True.
   - d. True.

Chapter 8

1.
A. pretérito perfecto; pretérito imperfecto; pretérito perfecto simple
B. pretérito perfecto simple; pretérito pluscuamperfecto; pretérito perfecto simple

2.
- a. True
- b. False. *Pretérito imperfecto* is the past tense in which the beginning or end of an action is not indicated.
- c. False. *Había hecho* is conjugated in *pretérito pluscuamperfecto*.
- d. True

3.
- a. bailaban
- b. cantaba
- c. soñaba
- d. estudiábamos

4. había perdido; había tenido; había plantado; habían entrado; había sido; había nacido.

5. María <u>estaba</u> abriendo las persianas de su tienda, como todas las mañanas, cuando <u>entró</u> un cliente nuevo. <u>Era</u> un hombre al que nunca <u>había visto</u> antes, aunque algo en su cara le <u>resultaba</u> familiar. <u>Tenía</u> un tupido bigote bajo la gran nariz.

—¡Buenos días! ¿En qué lo puedo ayudar? —<u>preguntó</u> María.

—Quiero un café grande, por favor —<u>pidió</u> el hombre, mientras <u>jugaba</u> con su bigote.

María se <u>dirigió</u> hacia la cafetera y <u>empezó</u> a hacer el café. Mientras lo <u>preparaba</u>, <u>notó</u> que la voz del hombre también le <u>sonaba</u> conocida.

—Disculpe, ¿nos <u>hemos visto</u> antes?

Entonces, con una sonrisa, el hombre se <u>quitó</u> el bigote de la cara. <u>Era</u> un bigote falso, por supuesto. María <u>dejó</u> el café sobre el mostrador, incrédula.

—¿Eduardo? —<u>preguntó</u>—. ¡Qué bonita sorpresa me <u>has dado</u>!

Chapter 9

1.
   a. Dice que en el futuro cada familia tendrá un cine en su propia casa.
   b. Porque la tarea de matemáticas sería mucho más sencilla.
   c. En el puesto de automóviles.
   d. De que en el futuro no hará falta trabajar.
2. diré; haré; iré; será; bajaré; tomaré; viajaré; serán
3. Match each pronoun with the corresponding conjugation of the auxiliary verb *haber* to form the *futuro compuesto* tense.
   1. yo: habré
   2. tú: habrás
   3. él/ella: habrá
   4. nosotros/nosotras: habremos
   5. vosotros/vosotras: habréis
   6. ellos/ellas: habrán
4.
   a. futuro compuesto.
   b. futuro simple.
   c. futuro simple.
   d. futuro compuesto.
5.
   a. True.
   b. False. *Presente simple* is used to talk about an action that is currently taking place.
   c. True.
   d. False. *Condicional compuesto* is conjugated with the verb *haber*.

Chapter 10

1. sobre; a; del; por; durante; para; a; a; de; desde; a; de; en; de; de; para; a; de; para; sobre; de; con; por; para.
2.
    a. False. There are many possible translations for each Spanish preposition.
    b. False. *Sin* is a preposition.
    c. True.
    d. True.
3.
    a. al; entre; y.
    b. desde; hasta; en.
    c. según.
    d. sino.
4.
    a.
    b.
    c.
    d.
5. vender gato por liebre; tiene que ver con eso; habla hasta por los codos; tiraba la casa por la ventana; está como una cabra; apodo sin pies ni cabeza.

Chapter 11

1.
    a. Estaba atendiendo a una de sus vacas.
    b. Veterinario.
    c. Tenía un problema estomacal. Se soluciona con un poco de medicación.
    d. Porque había vuelto a su casa a buscar una linterna.

2.
- a. ¿Cómo se siente Lucía?
- b. ¿Quién es él?
- c. ¿Dónde están los chicos?
- d. ¿Cuándo fue la última vez que viste a Tomás?

3.
- a. True.
- b. True.
- c. True.
- d. False. They are invariable, i.e., they are always written in the same way.

4. Disculpe; podría; por favor; gustaría.

5. Florencia mira el reloj. <u>No</u> es tan temprano como pensaba. Si <u>no</u> se apresura, llegará tarde al trabajo. Se sube a su coche y, como hay mucho tráfico, decide tomar una ruta alternativa. <u>Jamás</u> ha ido por esa zona. No parece haber <u>nada</u> por allí: es una calle desierta. <u>No</u> hay ningún coche y <u>tampoco</u> hay <u>nadie</u> caminando. ¡<u>Ni siquiera</u> tiene que esperar, porque <u>no</u> hay <u>ningún</u> semáforo! Llega a su trabajo más temprano que de costumbre. Ahora, ya sabe qué ruta debe tomar cada día.

Chapter 12

1.
- a. Moreno le preguntó qué le había dicho Sánchez.
- b. García le respondió que no le iba a creer.
- c. Le dijo que no dijera tonterías.
- d. Le preguntó qué opinaba Obrador.

2.
- a. False. Direct and indirect speech can also be used to reproduce something you have said.
- b. True.
- c. False. Em-dashes and quotation marks are used in Spanish to indicate direct speech.
- d. True.

3.
- a. se llamaba.
- b. respondió.
- c. había quedado asentado.
- d. se dedicaba.
- e. era.
- f. preguntó.

4.
- a. que.
- b. qué.
- c. que.
- d. si.

5. _____

Final Quiz

1.
- a. True.
- b. True.
- c. False.
- d. True.

2.
- a. Tú estás caminando.
- b. Ella está durmiendo.
- c. Nosotros estamos saliendo.
- d. Vosotros estáis dibujando.

3. hiciste; tenía; fui; era; hacía; había llovido; habías llevado; he dejado

4. hará - ayudarán - llevarán - se encargará - irán - _____

5.
- a. Condicional simple.
- b. Condicional compuesto.

    c. Condicional compuesto.
    d. Condicional simple.
6.
    a. con.
    b. de.
    c. durante.
    d. para.
7.
    a. <u>porque</u>: conjunción subordinante.
    b. <u>y</u>: conjunción coordinante.
    c. <u>aunque</u>: conjunción subordinante.
    d. <u>u</u>: conjunción coordinante.
8. irse por las ramas: to beat around the bush
   hablar hasta por los codos: to talk somebody's head off
   dar gato por liebre: to give a pig in a poke
   estar como una cabra: to be completely mad

9.
    a. cómo.
    b. cómo/dónde.
    c. quién.
    d. qué.
10.
    a. False. Indirect speech consists of interpreting and rewriting someone else's or your own message.
    b. True.
    c. True.
    d. False. Direct speech is the reproduction of a message in the same way in which it was said, without alterations or interpretations.

Here's another book by Lingo Publishing that you might like

Free Bonuses from Cecilia Melero

Hi Spanish Learners!

My name is Cecilia Melero, and first off, I want to THANK YOU for reading my book.

Now you have a chance to join my exclusive Spanish language learning email list so you can get the ebooks below for free as well as the potential to get more Spanish books for free! Simply click the link below to join.

P.S. Remember that it's 100% free to join the list.

Access your free bonuses here:
https://livetolearn.lpages.co/spanish-learners/

Made in the USA
Middletown, DE
27 May 2025